Twayne's English Authors Series

EDITOR OF THIS VOLUME

Sarah W. R. Smith

Tufts University

Thomas Campbell

TEAS 227

Thomas Campbell

THOMAS CAMPBELL

By MARY RUTH MILLER

North Georgia College

TWAYNE PUBLISHERS

A DIVISION OF G. K. HALL & CO., BOSTON

Copyright © 1978 by G. K. Hall & Co.

Published in 1978 by Twayne Publishers,
A Division of G. K. Hall & Co.
All Rights Reserved

Printed on permanent/durable acid-free paper and bound
in the United States of America

First Printing

PR
4414
m5

Library of Congress Cataloging in Publication Data

Miller, Mary Ruth.
Thomas Campbell.

(Twayne's English authors series ; TEAS 227)
Bibliography: pp. 157-61
Includes index.
1. Campbell, Thomas, 1777-1844—Criticism and
interpretation.
PR4414.M5   821'.7   78-18773
ISBN 0-8057-6728-2

Parentibus meis, maximis cum gratiis summo tum amore.

Contents

About the Author

Since 1976 Mary Ruth Miller has been Professor of English and Head of the English Department at North Georgia College in Dahlonega, Georgia. For nine years previously she held the same position at Tennessee Wesleyan College; she has also taught at Florida Southern College and Reinhardt College. A native Floridian, she received her A.B. from Florida State University, her M.A. from George Peabody College for Teachers, and her Ph.D. from Duke University, where she wrote a dissertation on *The Crimean War in British Periodical Literature, 1854–1859*, under the direction of Professor Lionel Stevenson. She has done additional summer study at Columbia University, the University of Southern California, the Shakespeare Institute at Stratford-upon-Avon, England, and the University of Edinburgh, Scotland. Her articles have appeared in *The Colleague* of Florida Southern College and the *ADE Bulletin*, and she has had a professional paper abstracted in the *South Atlantic Bulletin*. Currently she is working further on Thomas Campbell and on the Crimean War in literature. Additional biographical information is available in *Who's Who of American Women, Who's Who in the South and Southwest*, and the *Directory of American Scholars*.

Preface

Thomas Campbell was a humanitarian poet in a transitional position between Classicism and Romanticism. He enjoyed great popularity for a time, but before his death he had been relegated to second place among classic English authors—a judgment that still prevails. Today we read him for his place in poetic tradition and for his handful of good poems and lines that still evoke our deeper feelings.

Rather than contend against the changing public taste in poetry, Campbell sacrificed much of his time and energy to write prose for an income. His books and articles, both original and edited, responded to the demands of a growing reading public. For ten years he was editor of the *New Monthly Magazine,* one of the literary periodicals that were multiplying rapidly during his lifetime. In addition to his writing, Campbell took an active part in educational and humanitarian affairs. These involvements, together with personal sorrow, disease, and lack of discipline, slowed his productivity as a poet.

In Chapters 2 through 5, this study examines the merits and demerits of Campbell's poetry, introducing to the modern reader most of his poems, many of which are no longer familiar. The few not included are trivial, juvenile, or translations. Chapter 6 discusses all of the book-length prose works. Of his known periodical articles, however, space has permitted only a sampling. For both the prose and the major poems, excerpts from Campbell's major contemporary critics provide the perspective of literary history in accounting for his decline in popularity. Many of these critics, often well-known persons protecting themselves by anonymity, were so perceptive in their appraisals that their judgments have stood the test of time. Others, writing from a political bias, hurt Campbell's reputation by either excessive praise or vehement attack.

Chapter 1 presents Campbell the man in relation to his writing. Because his letters provide biographical interest and authenticity, I have made extensive use of the definitive *Life and Letters* edited by William Beattie. Yet Beattie is not objective. As Campbell's medical doctor, friend, and executor, performing a "labor of love" only three and a half years after the poet's death, he had to respect privacy and propriety. Today, however, many of the original letters he loyally edited are still available in British and American libraries. From my access to them I have been able to reveal for the first time the health problem that contributed largely to Campbell's decline as a writer and to his disparagement by his acquaintances.

Chapter 7 estimates Campbell today, summarizes the tensions in his life and poetry, and briefly relates him to his contemporaries. It is not an attempt to resurrect him, but it is a plea for a more impartial judgment than many of his past critics have been able to make.

In recognition of the bicentennial of Campbell's birth the reprint companies have brought out his poetry, some of his prose works, and Beattie's volumes. Thus, the rereading of Campbell is possible.

My pursuit of Campbell materials has led me to a number of libraries. Special thanks go to my friends in the Perkins Library of my alma mater, Duke University, for numerous interlibrary loan and reference services and for permission to return as a visiting scholar in the summer of 1975 to complete my volume; to the staff of the Merner-Pfeiffer Library of Tennessee Wesleyan College for patient assistance with many interlibrary loans; and to the University of Tennessee for use of its library resources. For the kind efficiency of their professional personnel in helping me gain access to their valuable manuscripts, I am indebted to the National Library of Scotland; the British Museum; the Bodleian Library of Oxford University; the Trinity College Library of Cambridge University; the libraries of the University of Edinburgh, the University of Glasgow, the University of London, and University College London; the Henry E. Huntington Library; the Folger Shakespeare Library; and the Houghton Library of Harvard University. To all of the many other libraries that have responded to loan requests, I am grateful.

Finally, I wish to express my thanks to Professor Sylvia E. Bowman for her patience with a slow writer and to my expert typist, Ruby M. Bailey, for the dedicated care with which she prepared my final manuscript. To the late Professor Lionel Stevenson I am obligated for the long-term loan of his copy of Beattie's volumes and for valuable training in the skills of literary research.

MARY RUTH MILLER

Chronology

1756   January 12: marriage of Alexander Campbell and Margaret Campbell in Glasgow, Scotland.

1777   July 27: birth of Thomas Campbell, youngest of eleven children, in Glasgow.

1785   October: entered the Grammar (High) School of Glasgow.

1791   October: entered the University of Glasgow for the first of five, six-month sessions he attended.

1795   Summer: spent on the Island of Mull as a tutor.

1796   Summer: spent as a tutor in Argyllshire. Began "The Pleasures of Hope."

1797   Worked in Edinburgh tutoring, studying, and writing.

1798   November: completed "The Pleasures of Hope" and sold the copyright for sixty pounds.

1799   April 27: "The Pleasures of Hope" published, along with several other poems.

1800   Went to Germany for travel, study, and writing.

1801   Wrote "Ye Mariners of England" and several other poems sent to *The Morning Chronicle*. With alarms of war, left Germany for London. Death of his father. Returned to Edinburgh. Engaged in literary hackwork. Wrote "Hohenlinden" and "Lochiel's Warning."

1802   Compiling the *Annals of Great Britain*.

1803   February 6: returned to London. Seventh edition of "The Pleasures of Hope" published with additional poems. Married his second cousin, Matilda Sinclair, October 10.

1804   July 1: birth of son, Thomas Telford. Moved to Sydenham Common, Kent. Completed "Lord Ullin's Daughter" and wrote first draft of "Battle of the Baltic." Also wrote for newspapers and worked on the *Annals*.

1805   June: birth of son, Alison. Awarded a government pension of two hundred pounds a year. Subscription edition of poems published.

1809   Published "Gertrude of Wyoming." Wrote "O'Connor's Child."

1810   Death of son Alison.

1811   Portrait painted by Sir Thomas Lawrence.

1812   February 24: death of his mother. April 24: gave his first lecture on poetry at the Royal Institution in London.

1815   Received a legacy of five thousand pounds.

1817   Visited by Washington Irving.

1818   Lectured at the Liverpool Institution.

1819   Published *Specimens of the British Poets.* Visited by Byron. Lectured in Birmingham.

1820   Lectured again at the Royal Institution. Visited Germany and Holland. Became editor of *The New Monthly Magazine.*

1821   Moved from Sydenham to London. Assumed duties with the *New Monthly.* Realized son Thomas mentally ill.

1823   Wrote "The Last Man."

1824   Published "Theodric."

1825   February 9: published in the *Times* his proposal for a university in London. Visited Germany to study the Berlin University system.

1826   November 15: elected Lord Rector of Glasgow University.

1827   November 14: reelected Lord Rector.

1828   May 9: death of his wife. Reelected Lord Rector in November.

1829   Formed the Literary Union. Students founded a Campbell Club. Ill-health chronic.

1830   Gave up editorship of the *New Monthly.*

1831   Became editor of *The Metropolitan.* Began *Life of Mrs. Siddons.*

1832   Ended his work with *The Metropolitan.* Formed Polish Literary Association.

1834   Published *Life of Mrs. Siddons.* Went to Algiers. Received a legacy of a thousand pounds.

1835   Returned from Algiers and began publishing *Letters from the South* in the *New Monthly.*

1837   Edited *The Scenic Annual.*

1838   Published an edition of Shakespeare and began *Life of Petrarch.*

1841   Published *Life of Petrarch.*

1842   Published "The Pilgrim of Glencoe" and other poems.

1843   Received two legacies totaling a thousand pounds. Published a new edition of his poems. Moved with his niece to Boulogne, France.

1844   June 15: death in Boulogne. July 3: burial in Poets' Corner in Westminster Abbey.

CHAPTER 1

"The Bard of Hope": Thomas Campbell

I Early Life

THOMAS Campbell was a native of Scotland, born in Glasgow July 27, 1777, to Alexander and Margaret Campbell, the youngest of their eleven children. His father, sixty-seven the year of the poet's birth, was a descendant of an Argyllshire family that prided itself on tracing its lineage back to the Normans.

As a young man, Alexander Campbell went to America and became a businessman in Falmouth, Virginia. Later he returned to Glasgow, where he and Daniel Campbell (no relation) established a profitable business trading in Virginia tobacco. Alexander married Daniel Campbell's sister Margaret, twenty-six years younger than her husband. The family prospered until the American Revolution put a stop to shipping interests and caused a financial disaster that greatly affected the life of the Campbells' youngest son.

The boy Thomas, described by his biographer William Beattie as "a lively, well-favored child, rather of a delicate than of a robust constitution, with beautiful expressive features, and a precocity of intellect,"[1] received much affection and encouragement from his parents and from his older sister Isabella, who recognized his gifted mind. The mother had taste, refinement, strength of mind and character, good managerial abilities, and a love for literature and music that she instilled in her children. Although she was sometimes severe, her manner was offset by the indulgence and equanimity of the father. Alexander Campbell was religious, loyal to the Kirk of Scotland. He loved music, especially naval songs, read widely, and knew well several of the leading thinkers of his day, including Thomas Reid and the economist Adam Smith, both professors of moral philosophy at the University of Glasgow. (The poet was named for

Dr. Reid, who baptized him.) The differences in temperament between the parents are observable in the later attitudes and habits of their famous son.

At the age of eight, Thomas was sent to the grammar school of David Allison, where he soon became head of his class. His proficiency in translating the Greek and Latin poets, required as school exercises, led to an enthusiasm for the classics that he retained for the rest of his life; this early enthusiasm became a major influence on the style of his own poetry. At one time during his early school days he contracted a serious illness and was sent to the country to recuperate. The rustic scenery he enjoyed there contributed to the poetry that he began writing by the time he was ten. Lasting personal traits that developed during his school days include opposition to unfairness, generosity to strangers, and kindheartedness. Then as later he enjoyed playing, exercising his wit, and forming friendships. The praise he received from both his family and his schoolmaster, who expected great things from him, boosted his youthful confidence.

In October 1791, when he was fourteen, Campbell entered Glasgow University for the first of five, six-month sessions he attended. During his college years he continued studying the Greek and Latin writers and won several prizes for his translations, along with awards for his own poems. Among the English authors he read, John Milton was a favorite; others, whose influence on him is evident, were Pope, Thomson, Gray, Goldsmith, and Burns. Participating in literary societies and debating clubs contributed to a lifelong interest in founding organizations for literary, social, and charitable purposes. As he watched the Glasgow militia exercise on the college green, his lasting fascination with the military began. Part of his study time he had to spend tutoring younger boys in order to aid the family's finances.

The nature of his education greatly affected Campbell's future. He prepared for no profession and seems to have contented himself with literary prizes instead of completing requirements for a degree. Mathematics he disliked, but along with Greek he enjoyed classes in law, logic, and moral philosophy—a broad area including psychology, theology, political science, and economics that strongly influenced the themes of his poetry. A member of his logic class was John Wilson ("Christopher North"), later a professor of moral philosophy at Edinburgh University, who as the principal contributor to *Blackwood's Magazine* frequently wrote about Campbell. For Campbell the university was an eclectic experience providing a general education and an awakened, questioning mind. Very significant in their influence were three great liberal professors: Thomas Reid, John Anderson, and John Millar. Millar, a brilliant lecturer in law, especially helped set the course of Campbell's lifelong Whiggism.

During his college days, Scots were taking sides for or against the French Revolution. Liberals excited by the need for changes at home included Thomas Muir, a young Edinburgh advocate who had been one of Millar's students. He was a chief founder of the Scottish Friends of the People—societies that advocated parliamentary reform and extension of the franchise, believing in Thomas Paine's *Rights of Man*. After the bloodshed and massacres in France in 1792 and the French declaration of war upon Britain, when it became evident that Edmund Burke's predictions in his *Reflections on the French Revolution* were coming true, many Scots began to fear Muir and his friends as revolutionaries instead of reformers. Alarmed officials arrested them and, in what was commonly regarded as a very unfair sedition trial in 1793, had Muir sentenced to transportation to Botany Bay for fourteen years.

Young Campbell, excited about the situation, walked from Glasgow to Edinburgh for the trial of Joseph Gerrald, Muir's successor in agitation for reform, in March of 1794. The experience, especially Gerrald's speech of self-defense, made a lasting impression on Campbell, who called it " 'an era in my life' " (Beattie, 1:91). It was a kind of initiation experience into his lasting political principles. His new seriousness and his interest in the theme of hope are reflected in his "Poetical Essay on the Origin of Evil," for which he won a prize shortly after his return from Edinburgh. This passage in heroic couplets is typical:

> Man's feeble race, what countless ills await,
> Ills self-created—ills ordained by fate.
> While yet warm youth the breast with passion fires,
> Hope whispers joy, and promis'd bliss inspires,
> In dazzling colors future life arrays,
> And many a fond ideal scene displays.
> The sanguine zealot promised good pursues,
> Nor finds that wish, but still the chase renews:
> Still lur'd by Hope, he wheels the giddy round,
> And grasps a phantom never to be found.
> Too soon the partial bliss of youth is flown,
> Nor future bliss, nor Hope itself is known;

> No more ideal prospects charm the breast,
> Life stands in dread reality confessed;
> A mingled scene of aggravated woes,
> Where Pride and Passion every curse disclose!

> (Beattie, 1:97)

According to his sister, this "Essay" helped earn Campbell the appellation "the Pope of Glasgow" from his imitation of Pope's "Essay on Man."

After his father lost a Chancery suit that had been in litigation around thirty years, thereby adding to the family's financial misfortunes, Campbell in 1795 obtained a summer tutorial position on Mull in the Hebrides. His pride and sensitiveness are evident in the fact that on his way, at Greenock, he purposely neglected to visit his mother's wealthy cousin, Robert Sinclair, one of whose daughters he married nine years later. To his friend James Thomson, a fellow student who had moved to London, he wrote: " 'Mull, God knows, is a place ill-suited to rub off the rust of a dull temper. Every scene you meet with in it is, to be sure, marked by sublimity, and the wild majesty of nature; but it is only fit for the haunts of the damned in bad weather' " (Beattie, 1:124).

Campbell was primarily a city person. His "Elegy Written in Mull" describes his homesick mood, which another college friend, Hamilton Paul, tried to cheer by writing: " 'We have now three 'Pleasures,' by first-rate men of genius, viz:—'The Pleasures of Imagination,'— 'The Pleasures of Memory,'—and, 'The Pleasures of Solitude!' Let us cherish 'The Pleasures of Hope' that we may soon meet in Alma Mater!' " (Beattie, 1:129) Beattie speculates that this casual reference led to Campbell's inspiration for his best long poem, which he began soon afterwards.

While on Mull, Campbell continued his translation of Greek drama, wrote some verses of his own, and enjoyed visiting the neighboring islands of Staffa and Iona, where he stored up poetic imagery for use later. The great cave of Staffa particularly impressed him; so did the sea close around, wide and storm-tossed. At least two young women on Mull left their impressions in his poetry: "Caroline," daughter of a minister in Inverary who visited his hostess, and an unnamed "Rural Beauty."

During other summer vacation periods, Campbell explored various professions, seeking a congenial one. Law, theology, medicine, business—none was the answer. Lack of patronage, financial backing, or interest deterred him. For some time, he expected to join his three brothers who had gone to America, but that plan failed too. (One brother, Robert, a merchant in Virginia, married a daughter of Patrick Henry.) Neither did he achieve his Master of Arts degree, as he had hoped, according to one of his letters to Thomson.

Leaving the university for the last time in 1796, Campbell returned to Argyllshire as a tutor to the future Sir William Napier. " 'Lying dormant here in a solitary nook of the world,' " he wrote Thomson, " 'the present moments are of little importance to me: I must expect all my pleasure, and pain from the remembrance of the past, and the anticipation of the future!' " (Beattie, 1:152). He read, did a little writing, and preserved images from the beautiful scenery of the Western Highlands, as well as ideas, for poems: "Glenara," "Lochiel's Warning," and "The Pleasures of Hope."

Restless, he returned to Glasgow in 1797 and soon went on to Edinburgh, taking with him two translations from Euripides and Aeschylus which he hoped to publish. To support himself, he worked as a copying clerk in the Register House and in a law office. His good fortune was an introduction to Dr. Robert Anderson, author of *Lives of the British Poets*, who became his friend and mentor. Through him he obtained a commission from the publisher Mundell to do an abridgment of Bryan Edwards' *West Indies*—the first of many such tasks he was to perform for money.

Back in Glasgow, working on the abridgment, he spent some time with a nearby family, where he heard a young lady play and sing many of the traditional Scottish melodies. For some of these, Campbell attempted to compose original lines. The resulting "Wounded Hussar," suggested by a recent battle on the Danube, was published and soon became widely popular. Typical of the punctuation difficulties that were to torment Campbell all his life, the ballad contained a semicolon in the wrong place, which changed the poem's meaning, but he was not able to make the correction for several editions.[2] About this time also he wrote "The Dirge of Wallace," a work of which he was never proud, terming it "too rhapsodical" and never publishing it in the London editions of his works.

II *Success*

After finishing the abridgment and spending some time revisiting his favorite haunts in the west of Scotland, Campbell determined to migrate permanently to Edinburgh, where he considered his prospects better than in Glasgow. In the fall of 1797, he attended lectures at the University of Edinburgh, did compilations for the booksellers, and tutored in the classics to supplement his income. Beattie quotes Lord Cuninghame, who had been a student boarder in the Campbell home in Glasgow and knew Campbell well, as saying that during this period Campbell's favorite maxim was that " 'a man accustomed to work, was equal to any achievement he resolved on; and that necessity, not inspiration, was the great prompter of his Muse.' " Beattie adds that "he was now convinced that, to acquire independence, he must cultivate the native treasures of his own mind" (1:195). Writing seemed to be the only way he was ever to make a living. At this early stage he discussed founding a magazine in conjunction with his school friends James Thomson, Gregory Watt, and John Douglas, but the idea never got beyond the stage of hope.

Campbell's own memoirs of these months record: " 'And now I lived in the Scottish metropolis by instructing pupils in Greek and Latin. In this vocation I made a comfortable livelihood, as long as I was industrious. But 'The Pleasures of Hope' came over me. I took long walks about Arthur's Seat, conning over my own (as I thought them) magnificent lines; and as my 'Pleasures of Hope' got on, my pupils fell off. I was not friendless, nor quite solitary at this period in Edinburgh' " (Beattie, 1:195–96). Important among his early Edinburgh friends were Francis Jeffrey, later editor of the *Edinburgh Review;* Thomas Brown, afterwards successor to Dugald Stewart in the moral philosophy chair of the university; John Richardson, then an apprentice to a writer to the Signet, with whom Campbell formed a close lifelong friendship that was strengthened by Richardson's marriage to Campbell's cousin; James Grahame, author of "The Sabbath," and his sister, Jean Grahame; John Leyden, poet, antiquary, and linguist; Henry, later Lord, Brougham, with whom Campbell was associated in founding London University; and Henry Cockburn. During the summer of 1798, he moved his parents to Edinburgh.

By that fall, "The Pleasures of Hope" was ready to appear. Abandoning the idea of publishing it by subscription, Campbell, with the help of Dr. Anderson, made an agreement with the publisher Mundell, for whom he had worked. Mundell took a risk on an unknown author and bought the copyright for the equivalent of sixty pounds (two hundred copies of the printed volume in quires). Afterwards, until Mundell's death in 1800, the poet also received the equivalent of twenty-five pounds per thousand copies of each new edition. Campbell himself was willing to part with the copyright for a small sum because he needed money and because he did not anticipate his own success. Later he lamented the bargain, especially when he and Sylvester Doig, Mundell's successor in Edinburgh, disagreed over payments.

During the time the poem was being revised and proofread, Campbell was in a highly irritable and nervous state, and his friends encouraged and helped him as they could. Beattie says, "Dr. Anderson, who had pledged his word to the public for the high character of the Poem, was indefatigable in his endeavors to have it brought out wih *éclat*. He objected, suggested, and exhorted to such good purpose, that the work of polishing was continued by the author with equal diligence and success" (1:214). It was Anderson who encouraged Campbell to rewrite the opening portion of the poem, which he considered unsatisfactory. (The original beginning, which Beattie prints from the manuscript, is inferior to the revised version.) Finally, the work was announced on April 27, 1799. Dedicated to Dr. Anderson, the volume included "Specimens of a New Translation of the Medea," "Love and Madness—an Elegy," "The Wounded Hussar," "Gilderoy," and "The Harper." At the age of twenty-one, Campbell emerged to sudden fame, "the Lion of Edinburgh."

Beattie quotes an unnamed friend of Campbell's who judged the impact of "The Pleasures of Hope": " 'It was only three years after the death of Burns that Campbell made this powerful and effective appeal to the taste of his countrymen. His strains were not deeper or more natural in their tone than those of his immortal predecessor; but they were elicited from a different string, and fitted to awaken a different set of emotions. The same distinguished men who had hailed the arrival of Burns in the Scottish capital, were still living, and equally ready to extend their favor to his youthful successor' " (1:218–19). Dr. Anderson's enthusiasm for the poem was verified, and, says Beattie, "never, perhaps, was any author more surprised than Campbell at the success which responded to his first appeal to the literary public" (1:221). As the " 'bard of hope, liberty, independence, patriotism!' " (Beattie, 1:224), he had caught the spirit of his day. "No poem had ever met with a more flattering reception; it was quoted as an excellent epitome of sound morals—inculcating, by lofty examples, the practice of every public and domestic virtue; and conveying the most instructive lessons in the most harmonious language" (Beattie, 1:225). The poet, his friends, the Whigs, and the publishers were all highly gratified. For a second edition, soon called for, Campbell revised the title poem and added several new passages.

As Campbell's fame grew, so did his circle of acquaintances. He noted that his immediate patrons included Henry Mackenzie, author of the "Man of Feeling"; the Reverend Archibald Alison, the "Man of Taste"; Thomas Telford, the engineer; and Dugald Stewart, professor of moral philosophy and a scholar of international repute. He came to know Henry Erskine, poet and lord advocate; and Walter Scott, whom he had already met through Leyden, invited him to a dinner to introduce him to his friends.

Elated by the compliments accorded to the patriotic parts of "The Pleasures of Hope," Campbell soon conceived a new heroic theme: a poem about Edinburgh to be entitled "The Queen of the North." According to Beattie, "the Poet was to celebrate the glory and independence of Scotland, as recorded in history and tradition; to display, in a series of martial episodes, the characters and achievements of her great men; and by the powerful aid of painting, re-kindle in the national mind her ancient spirit of freedom and independence" (1:227). Unfortunately, Campbell never completed the poem, even though Mundell had been engaged to publish it and a landscape painter hired to do the engravings. The topic was unwieldy, requiring more research than Campbell ever accomplished; besides, he became lazy and moody, and after he had left Edinburgh for Germany, he could not remember the home scenery well enough. He wrote to Richardson for help with facts and descriptions, but no one else could do what Campbell himself needed to do. Neither could he succeed in using epic-type materials and dimensions for a lyric poem—an ode. Despite his concern about leaving his " 'honor unfulfilled,' " the poem was finally abandoned after only the introduction was written —a " 'parting apostrophe to Edinburgh . . . from ship-board by moonlight,' " as Campbell described it in a letter to Richardson outlining the poem (Beattie, 1:291). This type of unfulfilled expectation became a theme in Campbell's life—not that he continually aborted poems but that he failed to live up to the promise as a poet that his friends felt he had.

With his volume selling well and his reputation established, Campbell decided to broaden himself by travel, "to be uncaged from this insipid scene of life," he told Thomson.[3] To visit Germany, then an important literary center, was foremost in his mind, but he also wanted to see London. For a time he planned to go by London to spend a week and then cross over to the Continent, but his mind changed. His letter of explanation to Thomson, then in London, prophesies much about himself:

God help this light head & still lighter purse. I had two objects in view Germany & London & was fool enough to believe I could overtake them both but as Germany could not be laid aside & as a twelvemonths' ramble on the continent is no joke to the finances of a poet I have avoided the seduction of that great city the whore of Babylon the brothel of the whole world the galaxy of genius the panorama of the universe &c. &c. . . .

To see London to see Godwin McIntosh Mrs Siddons & yourself was to me a long cherish^d expectation but many fears intervened. I know my own Nature as well as the Lord who made me idleness dissipation engagements with book sellers too various & extensive to be completed for some years new acquaintances & new sights would have dismiss^d the little industry I possess in Edinburgh & must have reduced me in a short time to the fetter^d state of a booksellers fag.[4] London would have swallowed me up like a vortex & to get clearly away with the stock I now possess would have been impracticable. My traveling to Germany must have been delayed for *God knows how long.* . . .

Besides upon reflection I see the propriety of making my first appearance in London to the best advantage. At present I am a raw Scotch lad & in a London company of wits & geniuses would make but a dull figure with my northern accent & braw Scotch boos. I am not satisfied with my quantum of literary character but intend to write a few more books before I make my debut in London.

He mentions that his intention upon his return from Germany was "to set up a course of Lectures upon the Belles Lettres" perhaps in Edinburgh, but he was too restless to remain "any longer in one place." In this long letter Campbell illustrates in his own life his later line in "Lochiel's Warning": ". . . coming events cast their shadows before" (1.56).

Carrying various letters of introduction, Campbell sailed on June 1, 1800, from Leith to Hamburg, accompanied by his brother Daniel, who expected to engage in business in Germany or Belgium. He was well received in Hamburg by the British residents, but they advised him to change his proposed itinerary because of political and military dangers from the Napoleonic wars. Consequently, he went to Ratisbon instead of Jena and later, as hostilities permitted, made excursions into the interior, getting as far as Munich. Then he returned by Leipzig to Altona, near Hamburg, for he was unable to visit Budapest, Vienna, and other cities enroute as he had hoped to do. Neither did he get to meet Schiller, Goëthe, or Wieland. A special letter of introduction enabled him to meet the seventy-six-year-old poet Friedrich Gottlieb Klopstock, then Danish legate at Hamburg, and through him several other distinguished men. August Wilhelm Schlegel remained his friend for many years. While abroad

Campbell studied French and German, but was able to communicate rather well with his Latin. During his stay he also read the philosophy of Kant, which he found disappointing. German literature he liked better, especially the works of Wieland, whom he called a "perfect Poet."

Campbell planned for his friend Richardson to join him on the Continent; together they would travel and collect literary information that they could later publish. Many of Campbell's most enthusiastic letters from Germany were addressed to Richardson in anticipation of his arrival, but for family reasons, Richardson could not go to Germany until Campbell had returned. This unfulfilled scheme is typical of many Campbell conceived that failed through faults not always his own.

In Germany Campbell enjoyed the scenery and the excitement of military events, both of which became material for his poems. To Dr. Anderson he wrote very romantic descriptions of what he saw, nevertheless alluding to his " 'admiration of "the pomp and circumstance of war" ' " as " 'a vain unfounded sentiment' " (Beattie, 1:239). That summer the French captured Ratisbon, and Campbell witnessed part of the conflict from the ramparts close to the Scotch monastery where he was staying. In a letter to his oldest brother in Virginia he described what he saw:

"One moment's sensation—the single hope of seeing human nature exhibited in its most dreadful attitude, overturned my past decisions. I . . . indulged in what you call the criminal curiosity of witnessing blood and desolation. Never shall time efface from my memory the recollection of that hour of astonishment and expended breath, when I stood with the good Monks of St. James [Jakob] to overlook a charge of Klenau's cavalry upon the French under Grenier. . . . We saw the fire given and returned, and heard distinctly the sound of the French *pas-de-charge* collecting the lines to attack in close column. After three hours . . . a park of artillery was opened just beneath the walls of the Monastery; and several drivers that were stationed there to convey the wounded in spring-wagons, were killed in our sight" (Beattie, 1:240).

The scene of the dead and dying on the field became a memory that haunted Campbell. In his memoirs he called this period " 'the most important epoch in my life, in point of impressions' " (Beattie, 1:240). Some of his best poems resulted from it. One of them, "Hohenlinden," was based on Campbell's view of other battlefields, not of the battle of Hohenlinden itself; however, he had toured the area of Hohenlinden a short time before the battle there.

During his stay, Campbell experienced some of the problems and emotional states that often tormented him in later life: illness, financial worry, loneliness, self-doubt, melancholy, and uncertainty about the future. Homesickness compounded the situation. Campbell was a man who needed constant reinforcement and assurance from his friends. His most intimate letters, those to his friend Richardson, whom he called his "dearest Guardian Angel," reveal much about Campbell, who termed himself "a sad dependant [*sic*] wretch."[5] This letter, dated December 16, 1800, from Altona, Beattie edited to delete the passage where Campbell admitted to Richardson the "sad reason" for spending the winter in Altona instead of returning home: he had contracted venereal disease from "a sweet little creature a Jewess in Altona whom I visited for the last time to take an affectionate leave. . . . *Oh shame where is thy blush.*" The Jewess is presumably the one to whom he addressed his unfinished poem "To Judith" (written at Altona, 1800). This disease in its various stages following inadequate medical treatment caused Campbell's health problems later in life as well as those of his family. Beattie, even though he was a medical doctor, refrains from identifying Campbell's "malady to which he was more or less subject through life" (2:221).

Despite his numerous complaints about unproductivity, Campbell managed to write some of his finest poems in Germany. The best known is "Ye Mariners of England" (an alteration of the old ballad, "Ye Gentlemen of England"), which he finished in Germany, signed "Amator Patriae," and sent to James Perry, editor of the *Morning Chronicle*. In his Christmas Day 1800 letter to Richardson, he mentions having sent fourteen poems to Perry and intending to send others in fulfillment of a financial scheme he had worked out prior to leaving home. Some of these poems, including "Lines Written on Visiting a Scene in Argyllshire" and "The Beech-tree's Petition," he merely completed in Germany. "The Exile of Erin" was based on his meeting the Irishman Anthony MacCann in Hamburg. Among the other poems he sent to Perry were "Death of My Only Son," "A Song, Translated from the German," "Laudohn's Attack," "Ode to Winter," "Lines written on seeing the unclaimed corpse of a suicide exposed on the banks of a river," "Ode to Content," and "Name Unknown." He revised his "Dirge of Wallace," wrote "To Judith" and "Lines on

Leaving a Scene in Bavaria," and composed drafts of other poems not published or else published under titles different from those he lists for Richardson, for example, "Palinode." "Battle of the Baltic," "Hohenlinden," "The Soldier's Dream," and "The Turkish Lady" he either began or gathered impressions for writing. The quantity of Campbell's poetic productivity enabled Beattie to state that throughout his letters, "whenever his mind . . . [was] actively engaged on any new theme, languor, lassitude, and all those ills that a parturient fancy is heir to, . . . [were] subjects of frequent complaint; . . . [yet] however depressed in physical health, his intellectual powers were in full and perfect vigor" (1:319).

Early in 1801 the political situation changed, so that it became unwise for British citizens to remain in Altona, which was on the Danish side of the Elbe. Denmark, Russia, and Sweden all sided with France, and an English squadron sailed for Denmark to defeat this coalition. Campbell hastily took passage in a small trading vessel bound for Leith. It sailed past the Danish batteries and, after weather permitted, reached the open sea. His sight of these preparations for naval war inspired "Battle of the Baltic." Just after his ship departed from its convoy, it was sighted by a Danish privateer and chased into Yarmouth. Campbell landed there, took a seat in the mail coach, and proceeded to London.

Arriving on April 7 with only a few shillings in his pocket after he had aided a friend in Altona, Campbell was disappointed to miss his old friend Thomson, but his editor Perry came to his aid. Through him he met Lord Holland, who introduced him to Sir James Mackintosh, Samuel Rogers, and other leading persons. It was an exhilarating time. Looking back later Campbell wrote that Lord Holland " 'reconciled me to hereditary aristocracy' " (Beattie, 1:295). Soon, however, his joy changed to grief when he learned of the death of his father, whom he had planned to visit shortly.

When he reached Edinburgh, he was surprised to hear that he was being charged with high treason for " ' "conspiring with General Moreau, in Austria, and with the Irish at Hamburgh, to get a French army landed in Ireland" ' " (Beattie, 1:299). After convincing the sheriff that the charges were preposterous, he turned his attention to looking after the financial welfare of his mother and sisters, whose situation was " 'dismal enough.' " His method of aid was to set up an annuity to be paid from a subscription edition of "The Pleasures of Hope" and whatever literary task work he could obtain. As long as these family members lived, he contributed to their welfare, usually with self-sacrifice.

During the summer of 1801, Campbell enjoyed the literary society of Edinburgh, entertaining his friends with his German adventures. Lord Cuninghame noted that Campbell's radicalism had cooled. " 'He now expressed a decided preference for the British Constitution, was less impatient of change, and trusted, far more than he did a few years before, to the gradual and progressive amelioration of all our institutions' " (Beattie, 1:304). Still he remained a liberal. "Lochiel's Warning," which he completed at this time, elicited enthusiasm from his admirers, who predicted greater things than Campbell ever achieved. He basked in their warmth, but termed himself " 'poor little "procrastination Tom" ' "—an accurate epithet (Beattie, 1:329).

During the next two years he divided his time between Edinburgh and London, spending part of it with Lord Minto, whom he met through Professor Stewart. Minto, later governor general of India, acted as a patron to him, inviting Campbell to spend some time with him at Minto Castle in Scotland and at his home in London. Campbell, in return, was to perform a few secretarial duties, but most of his time was to be his own. He was able to go out into society and to meet a number of eminent people, including Mrs. Sarah Kemble Siddons, the famous actress whom he greatly admired and whose biography he was later to write. Despite Minto's kindness, Campbell chafed under his largely imagined loss of independence; he preferred other arrangements. For a time in London he lived as a guest of his friend Thomas Telford, the engineer, who helped and encouraged him.

Beattie and other biographers of Campbell have lamented his decision to move from Edinburgh to London as having a deleterious effect on his poetry thereafter. Yet the move was almost inevitable. As Beattie points out, "No professorship, no lectureship, no 'appointment,' was forthcoming" (1:307). Prices were high, and Campbell had to earn a living. Certainly London offered more opportunities for work with the publishers. One such task was *The Annals of Great Britain*, a prose historical work that Campbell's pride dictated must be anonymous. After a few months the excitements of London wore off, and Campbell longed for " 'the refined and select society of Edinburgh' " (Beattie, 1:316). Later still he expressed wishes to return to Scotland to live. Nonetheless he became a

Londoner, and afterwards even looked upon Edinburgh as "pragmatic" and "cold-blooded."

At this stage, Campbell seemed to be drifting with no particular goal in sight. A proposed book of travels proved impossible because of conditions on the continent. Tiring of his situation, he took advantage of a somewhat improved financial status, resulting from the successful sales of the seventh edition of his poems, to marry his second cousin, Matilda Sinclair, whom he had met some years before. The wedding took place on October 10, 1803, at St. Margaret's Church, Westminster, and the couple took up residence in Pimlico, where the bride's father had furnished them a suite of rooms. The marriage was a happy one despite the early misgivings of friends and family members who provided them with loans. At this time Campbell was still the poet of hope.

The Campbells had two sons—Thomas Telford, named for the engineer, born July 1, 1804; and Alison, named for the Reverend Archibald Alison, born in June 1805. In the fall of 1804, Campbell took a twenty-one-year lease on a small house in Sydenham, a suburb of London, where the family lived happily until 1821. In 1804, Campbell described himself as becoming " 'avaricious,' " desiring " 'to haul in from the bookselling tribe as many engagements as possible, of such a kind as will cost as little labor, and bring as much profit, as may be' " (Beattie, 1:380). His work included anonymous periodical articles on numerous subjects (even agriculture), work for *The Star* newspaper and *The Philosophical Magazine*, encyclopedia articles, and proposals for a collection of poets. At one point he discussed editing a magazine that John Murray was contemplating founding. He complained to Scott that his " 'poetical vein . . . [had] ceased to beat' " (Beattie, 1:417); yet he continued to write poetry. In 1804 he finished three previously begun poems: "Lord Ullin's Daughter," "The Soldier's Dream," and "The Turkish Lady." In 1805 he sent a draft of "The Battle of Copenhagen" to Scott for criticism; Scott's encouragement helped him revise and shorten it into "The Battle of the Baltic."

To compound his financial difficulties, Campbell was a very poor business manager, never seeming to know exactly how his resources stood. Even though he remembered what he owed, the balancing of expenditures with income and keeping an accurate account of his money were matters for which he had neither inclination nor patience. Many times this laxness caused him needless embarras-

ment in having to ask for loans. In 1805, his friends came to his aid
with a subscription edition of his poems, and that same year further
relief came with the grant of a royal pension of two hundred pounds
per annum for his lifetime. (By the time taxes and fees were
deducted, it never netted more than one hundred sixty-eight pounds
per annum, and this he shared with his mother and sisters.)

Another problem for Campbell that also exasperated his friends
was his work habits, explained by Beattie:

> His flow of thought was not rapid; and the extreme fastidiousness of his
> taste was a constant embarrassment to his progress. In writing he was often
> like an artist setting figures in mosaic—cautiously marking the weight, shape,
> and effect of each particular piece before dropping it into its place. Nor did
> this habit of nicety and precision diminish with experience; for erasures are
> more frequent in his later, than in his early manuscripts. He was rarely if ever
> satisfied with his own productions, however finely imagined or elaborately
> finished. Aiming at that degree of perfection to which no modern author,
> perhaps, has ever attained, his progress was not equal to his perseverance; for
> what was written in the evening was often discarded the next morning
> (1:398).

Strangely, though, he was very unwilling to make even needed
technical changes once a work was in print.

Mental depression and various forms of ill-health, frequently
detailed in his letters, also slowed Campbell's progress. Adding to his
health problems was the fact that overindulgence in alcoholic bev-
erages led to chronic alcoholism in later life.

In appearance Campbell was slight but well knit, with small, rather
boyish features. He had sparkling grey eyes, dark eyebrows, thin
lips, and an expressive countenance. From youth on he wore a brown
wig to hide his baldness. He was neat in dress and an animated
speaker with a slightly quivering voice and tense gestures.

Leigh Hunt, writing of his literary acquaintances in 1809, described Campbell as "a merry companion, overflowing with humour
and anecdote, and anything but fastidious," as he was in his poetry.
Hunt termed him "one of the few men whom I could at any time have
walked half a dozen miles through the snow to spend an evening
with."[6]

Campbell told Walter Scott, another convivial companion on
occasion, that he was considering a poetry anthology, and for a time
they discussed a collaboration, with Scott doing the ancients before

Samuel Johnson's collection and Campbell editing the moderns after Johnson's. Their plans and terms were too great to suit the booksellers, however, and the joint project was abandoned. Scott became busy with other writing, but he encouraged Campbell to continue with the idea. Finally, in 1806, Campbell reached an agreement with John Murray to revise Johnson's *Lives of the Poets*, with selections from the works of each poet. Even though he continued the work he had already tentatively begun, it was 1819 before his *Specimens of the British Poets* was published in seven volumes, with an introductory "Essay on English Poetry," selections from the poems, lives of the poets, and remarks about them. Delaying factors besides Campbell's work habits included his difficulties in obtaining the books he needed to consult, other works progressing at the same time, and family problems.

In 1809 he published *Gertrude of Wyoming*, including with it "Ye Mariners of England," "Battle of the Baltic," "Glenara," and "Lord Ullin's Daughter." Most of his critics agree that this volume marks the end of Campbell's creative period. Only occasional pieces of merit appeared thereafter. During the composition of *Gertrude* in 1808, Campbell described himself as being " 'in high love with the work' " (Beattie, 1:499), but by the time he had finished the alterations, he was tired of the poem. His friend Francis Jeffrey criticized him for overly chastening, refining, and softening the work. Still, it remained Campbell's favorite.

III   *The Middle Years*

In 1810, Campbell suffered the tragic loss of his son Alison from scarlet fever, according to Beattie. His letters reveal the severity of his grief, from which he took some time to recover. In 1812, his mother died.

Besides his poetry and compilations, Campbell sought fame and fortune through another means: public lectures. His first intention upon invitation from the Royal Institution was to lecture on the Greek poetry he knew so well. Encouraged by his friends, he prepared a course of five lectures, for which he received a hundred guineas. Somehow, the five lectures of his contract became six as he outlined them in a letter:

"I begin my First lecture with the Principles of Poetry—I proceed in my Second, to Scripture, to Hebrew, and to Greek Poetry. In the Fourth, I discuss the Poetry of the Troubadours and Romancers, the rise of Italian

Poetry with Dante, and its progress with Ariosto and Tasso. In the Fifth, I discuss the French theatre, and enter on English Poetry—Chaucer, Spenser, Shakspeare. In the Sixth—Milton, Dryden, Pope, Thomson, Cowper, and Burns, are the yet unfinished subjects. It forms a sort of chronological—though necessarily imperfect—sketch of the whole history of Poetry. My endeavour is to give portraits of the succession of the truly great Poets, in the most poetical countries of Europe. I forgot to say that I have touched also on oriental Poetry" (Beattie, 1:542).

Scott commented to Joanna Baillie: "I hope Campbell's plan of lectures will answer. I think the brogue may be got over, if he will not trouble himself by attempting to correct it, but read with fire and feeling; he is an animated reciter, but I never heard him read."[7] After his first lecture Campbell, satisfied with his success, wrote to Alison that he " 'had taken no small pains with . . . [his] voice and pronunciation . . . and getting rid of *Caledonianisms* in the utterance' " (Beattie, 1:544).

The first course of lectures in 1812 was so successful that Campbell prepared a second course in 1813, also given at the Royal Institution. For his lectures, he used some of the materials he was preparing for his *Specimens of the British Poets,* causing Murray to hesitate about publication of the *Poets;* however, the two worked out the matter satisfactorily so that the lectures might also be published later.

Accepting other invitations, Campbell repeated his extended lectures at the new institution in Liverpool and afterwards in Birmingham. There he enjoyed a visit with James Watt, the aged inventor and father of his school friend Gregory Watt who at his early death had left Campbell a legacy of a hundred pounds. Campbell enjoyed lecturing, even perceiving that it " 'is likely to be my *métier*' " (Beattie, 2:96). Difficulties with his respiratory system, however, combined later with family problems to cause him to decline tempting invitations to Glasgow and Edinburgh, but he did give some additional lectures in London in 1820.

After the fall of Napoleon in 1814, Campbell, along with many other Englishmen, crossed the Channel to France. He visited his brother Daniel in Rouen and proceeded to Paris, where he enjoyed touring the Louvre with Mrs. Siddons and made valuable social contacts at the home of Madame de Staël, whom he had already met in London.

In 1815 his highland cousin, MacArthur Stewart of Ascog, died, leaving Campbell a legacy that amounted to nearly five thousand pounds, "in life-rent, and to his children in fee" (Beattie, 2:49).

When his *Poets* finally came out, while he was lecturing in Birmingham in 1819, its favorable reception encouraged Campbell to prepare his lectures for publication. He gradually did so, printing them in the *New Monthly Magazine* between 1821 and 1826.

Another result of his publication of the *Poets* was a controversy with William Lisle Bowles, editor of an 1806 edition of Alexander Pope's works. In his prefatory "Essay on English Poetry," Campbell defended Pope against the criticisms of Bowles, who censured the character of Pope and said Pope drew his imagery from art instead of from nature. Bowles replied to Campbell with a pamphlet, *Invariable Principles of Poetry. . . .* Lord Byron, champion of Pope in "English Bards and Scotch Reviewers," soon became involved, and a pamphlet war ensued. Campbell, who had no resentment against Bowles and privately considered Bowles' characterization of Pope a good one, had the wisdom to bow out.

In 1820 Campbell revisited Germany, taking his family with him. In addition to renewing friendships, he collected materials on modern European literature for the lectures he intended to publish. More important, from his observations of the German universities, especially the new one at Bonn, which had religious toleration, he first conceived his idea of a London university.

When he returned from the continent, Campbell assumed the duties of editorship of the *New Monthly Magazine* according to an agreement signed with Henry Colburn, the publisher, prior to his departure. The initial three-year contract, beginning January 1, 1821, called for Campbell to " 'furnish twelve articles, six in prose and six in verse; the prose to contain the whole value and substance of the Lectures on Poetry, now delivering at the Royal Institution; the copyright to revert to the author, in like manner with all his own contributions published in the said Magazine.' " Colburn agreed to " 'pay Mr. Campbell five hundred pounds per annum, and to provide a sub-editor; to pay for all necessary contributions a fair and liberal price, with the exception of the twelve articles mentioned, for which the editor desires no remuneration, unless, from the great increase in the sale of the work, Mr. Colburn should feel it incumbent upon him to make any' " (Beattie, 2:105). What Colburn mainly wanted, and got, was Campbell's famous name as editor. Campbell, burdened by his son's education, was glad to have the salary. He also hoped the position would give him the needed impulse to publish his own writings more promptly.

Even before the first of the year, Campbell set about selecting his staff and soliciting contributions, especially from his old friends. Sydney Smith, already working for the *Edinburgh Review*, reminded him that a successful magazine needs more than wit and genius; it also needs diligence and discretion. Campbell succeeded in obtaining good contributions and was especially fortunate to find an able subeditor in Cyrus Redding. Public response to the magazine was favorable. Beattie, in his usual adulatory manner, says Campbell "found himself at the head of a literary brotherhood, every member of which was either known and respected for his abilities, or eager to distinguish himself under so popular a leader; and seldom has so much diversity of power, with so much unity of purpose, been directed to the pages of a monthly journal" (2:136–37).

The magazine, founded in 1814, chiefly as a political organ, became literary under Campbell's editorship. When he took over, the publication began a new series and changed its name from the *New Monthly Magazine and Universal Register* to the *New Monthly Magazine and Literary Journal*. Original articles, poetry, and reviews became its emphases.

After the novelty wore off, Campbell began tiring of editorial duties. On December 5, 1822, he wrote to a friend that " 'the Journal and 500£ a year, I have a decided partiality to retain, but fear it will be wrung from my pride rather than my inclination' " (Beattie, 2:147). In 1826, he complained about " 'this *olla-podrida* that sickens and enslaves me every month' " (Beattie, 2:187). Occasionally Campbell grumbled about the amount of reading he had to get through by publication deadlines and about the irksomeness of " 'answering the complimentary petitions of blue-stocking misses to insert their verses, "in consideration of my universal character for generosity and candor" ' " (Beattie, 2:150). Sometimes he yielded to importunity and in cases of poverty and distress allowed his feelings to get the better of his judgment. William Hazlitt, one of the writers for the *New Monthly*, accused Campbell of petting the magazine too much, thereby rendering it "more remarkable for delicacy than robustness of constitution," and by trying to make it faultless, causing it to lose "some of its effect."[8]

Cyrus Redding, who soon found that he had most of the work to do, points out many of Campbell's shortcomings as an editor in his two works of retrospect: *Literary Reminiscences and Memoirs of Thomas Campbell* and *Fifty Years Recollections. . . .* Campbell, he says, was concerned about his own reputation and felt personally accountable for opinions expressed in the articles the magazine published. When

Campbell's idleness or failure to heed publication deadlines caused the printers to use materials that he had not carefully read beforehand, Campbell found himself having to apologize for his oversights to someone who had taken offense at an article. Usually he was disorganized, and frequently he was careless about answering and filing letters and articles he received. While these charges are probably true, Redding seems at times to be glorifying his own work at Campbell's expense. Campbell, however, had great regard for Redding.

After Redding resigned near the end of 1830, Campbell had to take over more work than he had been used to. A mix-up with his new assistant resulted in the printing of an article embarrassing to Campbell. This occurrence was the final straw that caused his own resignation from the magazine at the end of the year. Campbell wrote to a friend that " 'it was utterly impossible to continue the Editor, without interminable scrapes, together with a law-suit now and then!' " (Beattie, 2:238). Shortly thereafter he stated his intention " 'to give up all literary labor, save *for myself,* and to adhere to writing a work that would [*sic*] not bind me to living in town, or any where, permanently' " (Beattie, 2:241). Except for Redding, he would hardly have lasted as editor for ten years. Yet today the *New Monthly Magazine* is regarded as one of the leading periodicals of its era.

The amount of Campbell's original work during the 1820s is not large. A number of short poems appeared for the first time in the *New Monthly* while he was editor. The best of these are "The Last Man" and "To the Rainbow"; others are "Reullura," "The Ritter Bann," "Field Flowers," and twenty-three more, several entitled only "Song" or "Lines."

His next long poem was *Theodric,* completed in 1824. Campbell sent the manuscript to a friend for criticisms, commenting that he was " 'rather in good heart about it, though not over sanguine' " (Beattie, 2:160), and he warned his sister not to expect too much from " 'a *domestic* and private story' " that readers would feel contained " 'nothing grand or romantic' " (Beattie, 2:162). Despite the initial objections he anticipated, he felt that the poem would in time " 'attain a steady popularity.' " Nevertheless, this hope proved to be only wishful thinking. The friend, unnamed, complained of obscurity that Campbell only partly elucidated, and the public reaction was generally unfavorable.[9]

During the years of his editorship, Campbell suffered two personal misfortunes, the death of his wife and the realization that his surviving son was mentally ill. When Thomas at fourteen was pronounced incapable of studying, Campbell attempted to educate him at home or with private tutors. The boy's violence and capriciousness did soften into eccentricity, but it took Campbell a long time, and Mrs. Campbell longer, to acknowledge that anything serious was wrong or that he needed professional help. Beattie calls the illness a "hereditary taint" because Mrs. Campbell's sister was suffering from a similar disorder, but more likely it was congenital syphilis showing its effects. After Thomas became unmanageable, the anxious parents took him to an asylum near Salisbury. There and in another asylum near Essex he remained, except for occasional periods at home, until after Campbell's death, when a "Commission on Lunacy" met and pronounced him to be "perfectly sane," despite some eccentricities.[10] Some of the most poignant passages in Campbell's letters relate to his anxieties about his son.

By the beginning of 1828, Mrs. Campbell, who had not been well since 1824, began to decline in health. Atrophy set in, a possible effect of syphilis, and her condition worsened. To Campbell's sorrow, she died on May 9, 1828. With her early death, Campbell's greatest steadying influence was gone, and his life thereafter deteriorated.

Two major events that gave Campbell lasting satisfaction occurred while he was editor of the *New Monthly:* his part in the founding of London University, and his election to the rectorship of Glasgow University.

From the time of his return from Germany near the end of 1820, Campbell nurtured the idea that a major university offering education to all without religious requirements should be founded in the metropolis. He mentioned the scheme to many of his friends and profited from their suggestions. Although he found that they accepted the need for such an institution more readily than the idea that the necessary funds could be raised, he had hope. Following a dinner at his old friend Henry Brougham's during which Campbell presented the project to a favorable audience, he sent a public letter to Brougham that was published in the *Times* on February 9, 1825. Then Campbell helped draw up a prospectus endorsed by many prestigious men, and a subscription campaign began. Meetings were held and pledges multiplied. Campbell wrote numerous letters and published "Suggestions Respecting the Plan of an University in London" in the *New Monthly Magazine.*

A university in London was an idea for which the time had come. Fortunately for the project, practical politicians like Brougham and Joseph Hume, who pledged to raise a hundred thousand pounds, carried it through to completion. Campbell made many suggestions and exercised himself greatly to keep theology out of the curriculum and to keep either the Dissenters or the Church of England from predominating. He termed the day the decision was finally made that the university would have no religious rivalship an eventful one in his life. The religious question thus settled, the workers knew by the end of the summer that the scheme would be realized.

To learn more about the German system and to collect additional facts and materials, Campbell decided in the fall of 1825 to visit the University of Berlin and study it as a possible model for the new one. Despite his weak health at the time, he enjoyed the visit, which included a reunion with Anthony MacCann, his "Exile of Erin," at Hamburg and a public dinner in his honor there. Two young Englishmen studying medicine at the University of Berlin helped him with translations, sightseeing, and various details, but they were concerned about his health, one of them noting " 'the too certain approach of premature decay' " (Beattie, 2:175). Others also observed his premature old age.

In a speech in November, following his return, Campbell stated that if the London University succeeds, " 'I *shall ask for no better epitaph on my grave,* than to have been one of its successful instigators' " (Beattie, 2:176). Gradually he assumed a smaller role, finding it necessary to resign from the council of the university in January 1828. Three years after the scheme was made public, the university opened its doors. The Anglicans, to offset the "Godless Gower-street college," founded King's College in 1828; it opened in 1831. The earlier "Godless" college, after overcoming various objections, including protests from Oxford and Cambridge, obtained a charter as University College, London, and together with King's College became the University of London in 1836.

For a time Campbell complained that he was not given due recognition for his role: Brougham was claiming full credit to further his political career. It was especially galling to him that John Cam Hobhouse, Baron Broughton, speaking at the dinner celebrating the laying of the foundation stone, gave all the credit to Brougham (at the time, Campbell was in Glasgow, involved with his duties as lord rector). Later Campbell and Brougham were reconciled, and today

Campbell is given full recognition for his efforts, with the University College displaying appropriate memorials.

The honor bestowed on Campbell by his own alma mater came in 826, beginning with the students sounding him out as to whether he vould accept the rectorship of Glasgow University if they elected him. Despite some problems of health and finances, he replied affirmatively, and he won the election by a great majority on November 15. For Campbell the victory was a timely compensation or disappointments in his writing and in his family. Flattered by what he considered the " 'crowning honor of his life' " (Beattie, 2:186), he ook seriously the responsibilities of the office, which at that time had become largely ceremonial, filled alternately with Whigs or Tories. The rector could serve as judge in serious matters of academic discipline, settling quarrels between students or between professors and students; he could also audit accounts and make recommendations for the general management of the university.

So well did Campbell champion the students that they twice reelected him, the last time against severe protests from the faculty and against the Tory Sir Walter Scott, who withdrew his candidacy after a contested vote. Campbell devoted a large amount of time to his office, making numerous trips between London and Glasgow and holding conversations on behalf of the students with the Royal Commissioners of Inquiry, then investigating Scottish universities. He published his inaugural address for distribution to the students and later, after faculty objection to his lecturing to them, wrote a series of "Letters to the Students of Glasgow," covering the epochs of literature, which appeared in the *New Monthly Magazine* in 1827 and 1828. He also awarded gold and silver medals for literary composition. His "dear boys" showed their appreciation by presenting him a large silver punchbowl that remained one of his prized possessions. Moreover, they formed a Campbell Club, which was both literary and political. The faculty awarded him an LL.D., but he never cared to use the title.

Because of Campbell's interest in students, his service to London and Glasgow universities, his love for classical and literary scholarship, and his ability to lecture, some of his friends thought he would be able to find happiness in a university professorship. Several times during his life they proposed his name, Scott once offering to help him obtain a chair at the University of Edinburgh, but Campbell's current circumstances or interests always discouraged the prospects.

In 1832, after the Reform Bill had passed, one group of friends, probably students, suggested that he run for Parliament as the member from Glasgow, but he refused to be a candidate.

IV Decline

Within a year of his wife's death there were rumors that Campbell would remarry. At first he denied them, but after the year of mourning had passed, he moved into a larger house, acting, says Beattie, "upon the suggestions of an amiable and accomplished friend, deeply interested in his welfare, and destined, as he fondly imagined, to 'restore him to the happiness of married life.' " Friends thought the step a prudent one, according to Beattie. "The lady was a woman of good family and fortune, and endowed with those virtues which give sanctity and security to the domestic hearth" (2:219–20). Typically Victorian, Beattie refrains from identifying the lady, but the poems and letters reveal that her name was Mary. She was a Tory, not young, and she had lived at Sydenham. Possibly she was Mary Wynell Mayow, member of a family of Campbell's intimate friends at Sydenham.

For some reason the marriage never occurred. What really happened Beattie does not say, but in a footnote he comments on the inconstancy of the poet in his loves. One "Amicus," writing reminiscences of Campbell for the New Monthly Magazine, says that the lady objected that marriage at their age would make both of them objects of ridicule; furthermore, Campbell's income was insufficient for her accustomed style of living. He comments that Campbell took the whole case bitterly to heart and never got over it.[11]

Various oblique references in his letters, in his poetry, and in published commentaries indicate that rumors persisted and that Campbell's interest in the ladies was lifelong. In mentioning his loneliness and lack of family, Beattie says later that "his last hopes, on a point he would not name, were blighted" (2:491). A reviewer in the Literary Gazette adds that Campbell "was always falling suddenly, deeply or desperately in love with somebody or another."[12]

To promote opportunities for fellowship and to relieve his solitude, Campbell formed a Literary Union in 1829 and remained active in it until 1843. For several years he served as president of the organization, which soon became more social than literary, providing companionship and a place to read and talk.

When Campbell gave up the editorship of the New Monthly

Magazine, he owed the publisher, Colburn, seven hundred pounds. Mainly to pay off this debt, he accepted an offer to head the *Metropolitan*, a new periodical that began in 1831. Cyrus Redding was again the working editor. After a time, Campbell was induced to purchase a third share in the magazine with a loan of five hundred pounds from the poet Samuel Rogers. Soon afterwards the publisher, John George Cochrane, was threatened with bankruptcy, and Campbell was greatly relieved, through the generosity of another partner, to be able to extricate himself from his financial involvement and to return Rogers' money. Eventually he paid off Colburn as well. The *Metropolitan* changed hands, coming into the ownership of the novelist Captain Frederick Marryat of the Royal Navy, whose family had been Campbell's neighbors at Sydenham. For a time Campbell stayed on as a salaried editor, chafing under the amount of time the job required under Marryat's direction and doubting whether he could agree with Marryat on the West Indian slave question. Toward the end of 1832, after Thomas Moore had joined the magazine, Campbell gradually severed his connection with it and devoted his time to other projects. To the *Metropolitan* he contributed his "Lines on the View from St. Leonards," seven other poems, and an article or two, according to Redding.

At the death of Sir Thomas Lawrence early in 1830, Campbell's friends and Lawrence's family urged him to write the life of the famous painter. The publishers also wanted Campbell's name attached to the work to deter other less known prospective biographers and to make the obtaining of materials easy, since Campbell's discretion could be trusted. Because Campbell felt a debt of gratitude for the many kindnesses Lawrence had shown him during the more than twenty years of their acquaintance—for example, the portrait Lawrence had painted of him in 1809 was his favorite—he agreed that a biography would serve both a public and a private duty.

Although he started immediately collecting materials and working on the book, going so far as to send a notice to his friends and to fasten one onto his study door saying he did not wish to be disturbed for the duration of his labors, he never completed it. In June of 1830 he abandoned the task to his friend, D. E. Williams, who had already been acting as his collaborator. Several reasons discouraged Campbell in his task: his chronic ill-health, his overly ambitious plan for the work, the fastidious work habits his concern about his reputation dictated, contradictions in the materials that he did manage to secure, his inability to find something in them to say, his lack of knowledge about art, and finally, the insistence of the publishers that he meet a prompt deadline.

Earlier Campbell had promised to write the life of the tragic actress Mrs. Sarah Kemble Siddons, who died in June of 1831. By the end of the year, after freeing himself from his financial entanglement with the *Metropolitan*, he began compiling the biography with his usual slowness, aggravated by illness and nervous anxiety to please the family of the "divine creature." His final editorial duties with the *Metropolitan*, and especially his work with the Polish Association, delayed him. By the end of 1832, he had finished an octavo volume and offered it to the publishers, but they refused the manuscript unless he made two volumes of what for him was a difficult subject— the external presentation of a great actress. At the end of June 1834, however, the revised work was published, with Campbell "nervously sensitive about its reception" (Beattie, 2:306) largely for the sake of his own reputation.

The first of July he set out for Paris, intending to visit sites of classical history in order to compile a work on ancient geography and to collect materials for an original poem. The Louvre and the King's Library attracted him for a while, along with the changes in Paris in twenty years' time. Then, much to the surprise of his friends, he changed his mind about going to Italy and determined instead to visit Algiers and write a book about that French colony. He explained to a friend that one day while working on his geography, he noticed on a map

"the ancient Roman city of Icosium—that corresponded with the site of Algiers. Its eventful history rushed on my thoughts, and seemed to rebuke me for dwelling on the dead more than the living. Is not the question of how widely this conquest of Algiers may throw open the gates of African civilization, more interesting than any musty debate among classic geographers? To confine our studies to mere antiquities, is like reading by candle-light after the sun has risen. So I closed the volume I was perusing, and with all my soul wished myself at Algiers!" (Beattie, 2:315).

" 'I blessed my fate,' " he added, " 'that I had not in youth exhausted the enjoyment of traveling.' "

Leaving Paris September 2 for Toulon, he crossed the Mediterranean in a merchant vessel, suffering from his usual seasickness. In Algiers, he declined the offer of living quarters in the townhouse of the British consul because he was a known Tory. Campbell declared he had brought with him " 'the character of a staunch *Whig* ' " and desired " 'to maintain the character of an independent English gentleman among the French officers,' " on whom he depended for information (Beattie, 2:317). He was delighted to find that his opinions were being quoted from the *New Monthly* and that a French army captain was translating his poems for publication. From Algiers he wrote to Richardson that he enjoyed " 'prancing gloriously on an Arabian barb over the hills of the white city,' " feeling as if his soul " 'had grown an inch taller' " (Beattie, 2:318). In November he complained of cold weather, illness, and financial worries, but he wanted to visit Tunis " 'in order to inspect the ruins of Carthage' " and added that he had found " 'some Roman ruins that are not mentioned by any traveller that I have read' " (Beattie, 2:321). He then spent two months among the native tribes to collect information, and he took several voyages along the coast from Bona to Oran and inland to Mascara. To his nephew he boasted: " 'I have slept for several nights under the tents of the Arabs—I have heard a lion roar in his native savage freedom, and I have seen the noble animal brought in dead—measuring seven feet and a half independently of the tail. I dined also at General Trizel's table off the said lion's tongue, and it was as nice as a neat's tongue' " (Beattie, 2:323).

When he returned to Paris at the end of May 1835, Campbell had an audience with the French king to give him a report on the colony, and back in London his African adventures made him a popular conversationalist. From October 1835 through June 1836, he published his "Letters from the South" in the *New Monthly Magazine* in nine installments, merely revising the original letters he had sent back weekly to a lady friend in England. Beattie notes a difference between the spoken and the written accounts, for in the published form, much of the sparkle of his animated conversation (aided, no doubt, by his favorite punch) was lost. In 1837, Colburn published the "Letters" in two volumes, with an editor adding an appendix to lengthen out the second volume.

While he was in Algiers, Campbell was surprised to receive news that his friend Thomas Telford had died, leaving him a legacy of a thousand pounds. This " 'providential windfall' " alleviated his financial worries and enabled him to enjoy his travels more than he might have otherwise.

In the summer of 1836, Campbell spent four months in Scotland, terming it the happiest visit he had ever made there. In Edinburgh, his friends honored him with a public dinner, and he was made a "freeman of the city." He stayed a fortnight in the Highlands refreshing his memory of the scenery and collecting materials for a new poem, "The Pilgrim of Glencoe." Again, his writing was slow. He was working on it in 1838, but did not complete revisions until Christmas 1841. The poem appeared in an illustrated volume in February 1842, dedicated to Dr. Beattie, who says he had caught Campbell's poetic imagination by reading to him one evening a passage from the history of clan Campbell. As with "Theodric," the critical reception was generally unfavorable, the minor pieces in the volume receiving more praise than the title poem. These included "The Child and the Hind," "Song of the Colonists," and "Moonlight." Campbell himself admitted that "The Pilgrim" had faults, but Beattie defended its beauties despite their "waning lustre" (2:426). Worse than the unfavorable reviews for Campbell was the poor sale of the volume: a major possibility for income had failed, while his expenses had doubled from the cost of the engravings. In the past, a new poem from his pen had been as good as money; now Campbell was worried about his independence in old age. The fact that at the time the book trade was universally depressed was no comfort.

Unable to rely on his poems for sufficient income during his last years, Campbell lent his name to several moneymaking projects. One was an 1838 edition of Shakespeare's dramatic works, for which Campbell wrote remarks on the life and writings. Another was the *Scenic Annual, for 1838*, which he edited. It included some of his poetry, notably "Cora Linn," but as he told his cousin William Gray, " 'It is got up for the sake of republishing some fine plates, and adding some new ones—the literary portion of which consists of merely notices affixed to each landscape. You will hear me much abused; but as I get £200 for writing a sheet or two of paper, it will take a deal of abuse to mount up to that sum' " (Beattie, 2:360).

Later that year he turned to editing a *Life of Petrarch*, left in manuscript by Archdeacon Coxe, but was unable to explain to himself why he did so, since it was " 'neither very pleasant, nor very profitable' " (Beattie, 2:369). As he progressed, however, he became more interested in Petrarch, whose sonnets he had considered monotonous and whose passion for Laura wild and half insane. Deciding that their affection was mutual, he told a correspondent that the love of Petrarch and Laura was " 'redeemed from its illegitimacy by its purity, its intensity, and its constancy.' " He defended Petrarch's passion as having " 'the spirit of conjugal devotion, without its ceremonies' " and concluded that because of his steadfast devotion, Petrarch was " 'an evangelist of faithful marriage' " (Beattie,

2:370). Finding Coxe's manuscript "stupid," he determined to start
over and write the *Life* himself, but as usual he was slow, and the
work became wearisome. Besides reading continental biographers,
he even took time to study Italian, so that he could read Petrarch's
sonnets in the original; moreover, in his youthlike zeal, he considered
a journey to Italy. As he tried to make his own work clear and
interesting, he enjoyed reading about the old Italian republics with
their leaders and battles. By the end of 1840, he had overcome
ill-health and lagging enthusiasm to finish it, but it was not published
until the middle of March 1841. Campbell joked: " 'The compositors
have slumbered over it; partly, perhaps, from the soporific matter of
the work' " (Beattie, 2:408).

Beattie attributes Campbell's subsequent interest in editing a life
of Frederick the Great to his seeing a theatrical comedy about him.
All he did as editor, however, was to write an introduction to the four
volumes, *Frederick the Great, His Court and Times*, 1842–1843.
Campbell also lent his name to a *History of Our Own Times*, "by the
author of The Court and Times of Frederick the Great," in two
volumes, 1843–1845. The second appeared after his death.

One of the driving forces in all of Campbell's life was
philanthropy—sympathy with suffering, and relief of distress. The
major recipients of his time, energies, and money were the Poles,
who were victims of partition and persecution, both political and
religious, at the hands of the Russians, Prussians, and Austrians. The
trial of Joseph Gerrald, which he had witnessed as a boy, aroused in
him strong feelings against persecution and denial of liberty, and in
"The Pleasures of Hope," he imagined that in 1794 "Freedom
shrieked—as Kosciusko fell!" (I, 382).[13] Also in that work, Campbell
saw the relation between the patriot and the poet:

> Yes! in that generous cause for ever strong,
> The patriot's virtue and the poet's song,
> Still, as the tide of ages rolls away,
> Shall charm the world, unconscious of decay!

(I, 461–64)

An uprising of Polish patriots in 1830 failed, leading to the exile of
about ten thousand soldiers and political leaders to France, England,
and elsewhere. The right wing political group of this "Great Emigra-
tion," led by Prince Adam Czartoryski, attempted to interest the
Western powers in the Polish question, while the left wing, in
alliance with international revolutionary groups, sought to instigate a

new insurrection in Poland. The insurrection failed and repression increased, resulting in the intensification of Polish national sentiment. The exiles abroad maintained a constant agitation. It was these people with whom Campbell became associated.

During his European travels in 1820, he met many of the earlier Polish exiles, whose stories revived his interest in their cause. Then in 1831, the news came that Warsaw had fallen; to Campbell " 'a brave nation is thrust a second time, assassinated, into her grave' " (Beattie, 2:240). Owning " 'my soul has been attached to the cause of Poland, from youth to age' " (Beattie, 2:241), he expressed his " 'grief and wrath' " in two poems, "Lines on Poland" and "The Power of Russia," both of them shaming England for failing to go to the aid of her suffering neighbor.

Besides writing poems, articles, and letters on behalf of the Poles, Campbell made speeches, sent a contribution of a hundred pounds to the hospital of Warsaw, endeavored to raise money, and formed a Polish Committee, which led to his organization of the Literary Polish Association in 1832 to support the old poet J. U. Niemciewitz and his fellow exiles. Another purpose of the association was to collect, publish, and distribute information about Poland to arouse and keep alive public interest in the cause; one of its outlets was a monthly journal for which Campbell wrote articles. The meeting chambers the committee rented turned out to be those where Milton had lived when he wrote his "Defence of the People of England," a fact that Campbell termed " 'singular.' " So completely involved was he in his exertions that one of his friends called him " 'mad on the subject of the Poles!' " (Beattie, 2:246). In 1833, Campbell, exhausted physically and financially, resigned the presidency of the association, but he continued giving to their cause until 1839.

The Poles themselves, ever appreciative, called him their staunchest friend in England, honored him in 1834 as the "Poet of Freedom" at a public testimonial dinner in Paris presided over by Prince Czartoryski, and later at his funeral scattered onto his coffin a handful of earth taken for the purpose from the tomb of Kosciusko. For Campbell, however, the " 'experience of human gratitude,' " as he expressed it (Beattie, 2:249), was reward sufficient.

Another cause in which Campbell interested himself in 1832 was that of German freedom. Relating it to the Polish question, he engaged in correspondence with German patriots, chaired a meeting of the friends of Germany, wrote "Ode to the Germans" for the *Metropolitan*, and received thanks from a deputation representing six hundred citizens of Frankfort and Hanau. His "Ode" was translated into German and set to popular music.

As might be expected, the slavery question also interested Campbell. He termed slavery " 'a curse and a crime, that cannot be too soon abolished' " (Beattie, 2:337). On the occasion of an American Negro's lynching, which he read about in the papers, Campbell wrote that he had with great difficulty refrained from making " 'a red-hot speech' " about it at the public dinner in Edinburgh given in his honor in 1836, presided over by his old friend John Wilson (Beattie, 2:343). Another time, upon hearing of an American atrocity, he wrote an epigram on the American flag, likening its stripes to the Negroes' scars. In July 1840, an antislavery congress was held in England. When Campbell attended a session and was invited to speak, he used the opportunity to praise " 'the philanthropists of the world' " whose object was " 'the *emancipation* of man, everywhere, from the thraldom of man!' " and stated, " 'The poetry of the world has always been, as it ever will be, on the side of liberty' " (Beattie, 2:500–501).

Other philanthropic interests of Campbell's ranged widely: from writing many complimentary verses to numerous letters of introduction and recommendation, patronizing dramatic talent, championing the cause of a convicted prisoner, aiding poverty-striken widows, and giving relief to needy people of various sorts. He supported Catholic emancipation in Ireland and the cause of freedom in Greece, Spain, and Italy. To raise funds for the relief of Spanish and Italian refugees, he undertook to edit a volume of gratuitous literary contributions. He helped promote an Association for the Encouragement of Literature, the main purpose of which was to assist needy authors in publishing their works. Many of his letters to fellow poets unselfishly sought help for persons he felt deserving. By nature Campbell was kind and sometimes overly credulous.

His great love for children found expression not only in his poetry but in his letters and deeds. Perhaps it was the loss of his younger son, his wife, and normal relationship with his older son that contributed to his literally doting on beautiful children as he grew older. Little girls he found especially irresistible. His "Lines on My New Child Sweetheart," written in 1841, begin:

> I hold it a religious duty
> To love and worship children's beauty;
> They've least the taint of earthly clod,
> They're freshest from the hand of God; . . .

> We love them not in earthly fashion,
> But with a beatific passion (ll. 1–8).

The subject was a four year old charmer he saw on a walk in a park. Failing to get her name and address, and unsuccessful in his later inquiries, he resorted to placing an advertisement in a newspaper describing himself and the child and giving the place and date he saw her, in the hope that the parents would identify themselves and permit him to see her again. To his disappointment, the replies he received were less than satisfactory.

In 1840, he spent thirty guineas for a picture of a gipsy girl painted by Eugenio Latilla that he was unable to resist after passing it daily in a shopkeeper's window. This picture is the subject of his poem "On Getting Home the Portrait of a Female Child, Six Years Old."

Later in life Campbell is frequently portrayed as a man "with his share of human foibles": sudden in passions, easily overpowered by wine, coarse in the stories he told.[14] Other commentators distinguish Thomas Campbell the poet from Tom Campbell the man, making derogatory remarks about the appearance and habits of the failing old man.

People who knew Campbell describe him variously as vain, sensitive, self-conscious, eccentric, impulsive, capricious, irresolute, dilatory, indolent, short in span of attention, querulous, and jealous of his reputation. He also had great conversational powers and was frequently a jovial host and a guest known as a merry companion. After his death there was a rash of "reminiscences" published in the periodicals, many written by persons who knew Campbell only slightly or only in his last years, and a number of them are gossipy and derogatory; yet for every unfavorable article, an adulatory one can be found. Often the admirers of Campbell as a person had to overlook some of his human weaknesses; and often the critics of his failures reveal their own misanthropy.

Like Coleridge, Campbell was fortunate in having a physician for a friend. Dr. Beattie had been physician to King William IV. Now he and his family frequently welcomed Campbell to their cottage in Hampstead to restore his health and spirits. The poet enjoyed these visits to the "Campbell ward," as he called it, from about 1833 on, when his future biographer noted "the progress of disease" (2:292).

In 1841, Campbell's benevolences to his niece, Mary Campbell, began to include himself. Mary, then seventeen or eighteen, was the daughter of his deceased brother Alexander, and Campbell had paid for her education. Now she was to become his housekeeper, and he told her mother he would " 'instruct her mind whenever she chooses' " (Beattie, 2:408), give her a new pianoforte, provide music and dancing lessons, and arrange for her financial independence after his decease by willing her all of his possessions. Anticipating an end to his loneliness, he leased a new house in Victoria Square, Pimlico, the area where he and Matilda had first set up housekeeping. Such extra expense Dr. Beattie considered unwise, but Campbell, ever hopeful, saw only the bright possibilities. During the summer before his niece arrived, he made a sudden trip to the baths at Weisbaden and Ems in Germany to seek relief from his rheumatism, but the uncomfortable journey did little good.

Back home, his niece joined him, and that fall he described her to Richardson as " 'a nice, comfortable housekeeper' " who so far seemed " 'well principled and amiable' " (Beattie, 2:424). "To my Niece Mary Campbell" expresses his gratitude to her, saying, in part:

> Thy playfulness and pleasant ways
> Shall cheer my wintry track,
> And give my old declining days
> A second summer back! (ll. 5–8)

(In later life, Mary married W. Alfred Hill, who edited the first important edition of Campbell's *Poetical Works* with notes and a biographical sketch.)

By 1842, with his poems selling poorly, Campbell became worried about his financial situation and determined to dispose of his house, which the neighbors by then were calling dirty, and retire to a place cheaper to live than London. Beattie states that "he might have had other motives," for "he had begun to feel the certain advances of old age" and had "private sorrows on which we have no right to speculate" (2:428). After considering several spots, Campbell decided to move across the channel to Boulogne, France, where he felt he could live and educate his niece more cheaply and where he hoped the sea air would benefit his health. Despite moving expenses, the difficulty of getting rid of his lease in Pimlico, and the objections of his friends, he and Mary departed for Boulogne in the summer of 1843.

Before he left, he wrote to Sir Robert Peel, seeking to become a candidate for the poet laureateship, then vacant after Southey's death. The prime minister forwarded his letter to the lord chamberlain and told Campbell he understood that the lord chamberlain was recommending Wordsworth for the position.

During the summer, the climate of Boulogne was enjoyable and the living expenses lower than in England, but by winter Campbell was complaining of cold winds and the difficulty of getting books from home through customs. He was working on a volume of ancient geography intended for school libraries which he planned to entitle *Lectures to my Niece.*

In 1843, Campbell's financial situation improved somewhat with a legacy of two hundred pounds from Andrew Becket, a dramatist who had been secretary to David Garrick. His sister Mary also died that year and left him around eight hundred pounds, much of it money he had sent to her for thirty years as an annuity.

Gradually his health weakened; and early in June 1844, Dr. Beattie, who was an executor as well as his medical adviser, together with Mrs. Beattie and Mrs. Beattie's sister, journeyed to Boulogne to be with him. The other executor, William Moxon, arrived June 13. Beattie even kept a journal of the poet's last hours, noting on June 9 that "organic disease exists in its worst form" (2:460). Death came June 15.

After some question about burial in Glasgow, Moxon made arrangements for Campbell's interment in Westminster Abbey, in the center of the Poets' Corner. The funeral took place on July 3, attended by a large group of dignitaries, including the recently resigned prime minister, Sir Robert Peel; the Duke of Argyll; the Earl of Aberdeen; Lord Brougham; several other members of the nobility who with the four just named served as pallbearers; and his old friend John Richardson. Contemporary periodicals, including the *Athenaeum* and the *Illustrated London News*, give accounts of the event.

Afterwards a subscription campaign to raise a monument failed to produce enough money to satisfy the sculptor, William Calder Marshall (who had worked on faith), and to pay a fee to the dean and chapter of the abbey. Another problem was that a base for the statue promised by the Poles could not be shipped out of Poland because of the internal situation there. Finally, however, after numerous delays and special arrangements, the monument was erected in 1855. The life-sized statue, depicting Campbell in his robes as lord rector of Glasgow University with a stanza from "The Last Man" carved on the pedestal, still occupies a prominent place in the Poets' Corner today.

CHAPTER 2

The Meteor's Flash: The Long Poems

I "The Pleasures of Hope"

CAMPBELL'S longest and first published poem, "The Pleasures of Hope," established his fame. Its 1,078 lines of heroic couplets in the tradition of Pope are divided into two parts, each a series of vignettes and abstractions on the theme of hope. Part I concentrates on the temporal or human level; Part II looks to the eternal or divine. Both stress the importance of anticipation as an essential human ingredient for inspiration, motivation, and consolation—for creating actual happiness. Themes include love, imagination, and amelioration. Several of the subjects of this discursive didactic poem were to emerge later as themes of separate works; for example, the American setting of Part I, lines 325–34, developed into "Gertrude of Wyoming."

Part I opens with the image of a rainbow arching over the hills on a summer evening and contrasts the appeal of the distant landscape with the near: " 'Tis distance lends enchantment to the view" (l. 7). As with nature, so with life: "we linger to survey / The promised joys of life's unmeasured way" (ll. 9–10). In these opening lines, Campbell exhibits not only the traditional attitude of a youth anticipating the future and the part in it he hopes to play, but he also falls into the practices of youthful poets, such as poetic diction: "Heaven's ethereal bow"; antiquated verbs: "hath been"; and frequent personifications: "Heaven's" and "Fancy."

Often he uses a rhetorical question and answer device: "Can Wisdom lend . . . / The pledge of Joy's anticipated hour?" (ll. 17–18). No. Wisdom "darkly sees the fate of man" (l. 19) and pictures Nature "too severely true" (l. 22). Another favorite device is apostrophe: "With thee, sweet Hope! resides the heavenly light / That pours remotest rapture on the sight" (ll. 23–24). Always a problem is point of view. From the general *we* in line 9, the poet moves to the personal

I: "I see the sister band, / . . . start at thy command, / And fly where'er thy mandate bids them steer, / To Pleasure's path, or Glory's bright career" (ll. 27–30).

In primeval times, Hope alone remained behind "when all the guardian deities of mankind abandoned the world," as Campbell explains in his analysis of the poem (p. 1). Hope was evident when the prophet's mantle descended on Elijah; now "Auspicious Hope" can reward, console, and give dreams to today's "wayworn pilgrim."

Hope, the "Angel of life," accompanies the pilot whose bark is "careering o'er unfathomed fields" (l. 56) as far as "Oonalaska's shore" and lends her visions to "the watchman's pensive soul" (l. 74) to help him recall "his native hills," "his cottage home," his beloved "Helen," "his children dear," and "his faithful dog" (ll. 75–86). (The scene in Burns's "The Cotter's Saturday Night" and the homecoming of Odysseus in the *Odyssey* are likely background sources for these lines. Goldsmith would also recognize the sentiment.)

Hope is "Friend of the brave"—the fighting man who "Hails in his heart the triumph yet to come, / And hears thy [Hope's] stormy music in the drum!" (ll. 99–100). A specific example of the aid of Hope is that to "the hardy Byron," grandfather of the poet, who had published an account of a shipwreck he had barely survived off the coast of Chile in 1741.

"Congenial Hope" kindles the passion of youth "to search the boundless fields of fame!" (l. 126). Like the Sibyl leading Aeneas through the underworld, she shows to youth the scientists Newton, Franklin, Herschel, and Linnaeus in their researches; the "admiring Plato" who recorded the works of "the Father sage," Socrates; and the Muses, who may inspire epic poetry like Virgil's, love poetry pleasing to Venus, tragic hymns like those of Orpheus, or "seraph words" like Milton's "to plead the cause of Heaven" so that "the living lumber of . . . earth / . . . receives a second birth / . . . And man, the brother, lives the friend of man" (ll. 184–194).

With a backward glance at Gray's "Elegy Written in a Country Churchyard," Campbell says that as a "Propitious Power" Hope can prophesy to parents "doomed to Poverty's sequestered dell" (l. 203) a better day, when their children will "yet assuage / Their father's wrongs, and shield his latter age" (ll. 211–212); their mother's "parted spirit" they will "soothe" by shedding "tears of Memory" over her grave. As the "playful innocent" child grows older, he "sits to hear / The mournful ballad warbled in his ear" (ll. 257–58) as "admiring Hope" looks fondly on the family scene.

A vague transition leads to a view of a prisoner, "The dim-eyed tenant of the dungeon gloom" (l. 268) who, aided by Hope, sees "his blazing hearth and social board" (l. 270) and finds that "virtue triumphs o'er remembered woe" (l. 272). The antithesis to Hope, "proud Reason," should not "chide . . . his peace" (l. 273).

The next picture is of the "wild maniac" who sings "to chide the gale / That wafts so slow her lover's distant sail" (ll. 277–78), in a merciful hope that he will return despite the fact that she has already seen his "shroudless corse" washed ashore. Now memory has "fled her agonizing brain; / . . . And aimless Hope delights her darkest dream" (ll. 284–88). (She may have suggested to Scott some of his later creations of madwomen.)

An equally pathetic picture is that of a homeless, friendless wanderer, unpitied for his past mistakes, who stops by a beautiful cottage and longs for one of his own where he would " 'no stinted boon assign / To wretched hearts with sorrow such as mine!' " (ll. 311–12). Sympathetic "Hope half mingles with the poor man's prayer" (l. 314).

From individuals the poet turns to society: "Come, bright Improvement! on the car of Time, / And rule the spacious world from clime to clime" (ll. 321–22). He sees civilization coming to "Erie's banks, where tigers steal along / And the dread Indian chants a dismal song" (ll. 325–26). Some day there will be flocks, shepherds, and the sound of "The village curfew as it tolls profound" (l. 334). Truth will put an end to "damnèd rites" of sacrifice and to barbarous hordes, and captives "From Guinea's coast to Sibir's dreary mines" (l. 342) will ask back "the image . . . that Heaven bestowed" (l. 346).

In the last sections of Part I, Campbell largely abandons addressing Hope and instead preaches to man, using vivid descriptions and narration of what man does to man. When he reaches the subject of Poland, he catches fire and writes one hundred twenty-four lines graphically portraying the hopeless defense of Warsaw against "leagued Oppression" by a handful of brave fighters under the leadership of Kosciusko. "Sarmatia [Poland] fell, unwept, without a crime; / Found not a generous friend, a pitying foe, / Strength in her arms, nor mercy in her woe!" (ll. 376–78). To Campbell, "Hope, for a season, bade the world farewell, / And Freedom shrieked—as Kosciusko fell!" (ll. 381–82). In a long part that he calls in the analysis an "apostrophe to the self-interested enemies of human improvement" (p. 1), the poet asks where the "Vengeance" of God was, and urges the return of the spirit of great heroes of the past like "the patriot Tell" and "the Bruce of Bannockburn," who fought for "Freedom's cause" (ll. 409–10). Hope opposes dark oppression and the tyrants who raise "War's polluted banner" (l. 437), but modern man seems content merely to read about past glories. "Hath Valour left the world—to live no more?" (l. 454). In this line and in lines 461–64, Campbell foreshadows his war odes, linking the poet and the patriot:

> Yes! in that generous cause for ever strong,
> The patriot's virtue and the poet's song,
> Still, as the tide of ages rolls away,
> Shall charm the world, unconscious of decay!

A long passage on slavery follows, with the outraged poet addressing the "degraded men":

> Trade, wealth, and fashion, ask you still to bleed,
> And holy men give Scripture for the deed;
> Scourged and debased, no Briton stoops to save
> A wretch, a coward; yes, because a slave! (ll. 485–88)

Man was not meant to be a slave to man—"Nature stamped us in a heavenly mould!" (l. 498). Then, a moving picture of the captive slave indicts the slave trade.

Finally the poet turns to India and devotes seventy-four lines to the exploitation of the "dominions of the sun," led by the "Nurse of Freedom," Britain. The minions of "Degenerate Trade" could "barter, with their gold, eternal shame!" (l. 570). Part I ends with the guardian spirits of India prophesying a day of vengeance. Brama [sic] will appear a tenth time and " 'chase destruction from her [India's] plundered shore' " (l. 597). " 'Love!—Mercy!—Wisdom!—rule for evermore!' " (l. 604), the guardian spirits cry.

Part II is more abstract and less developed than Part I; it therefore demands the reader's close attention to follow its thread. It begins with youthful rejoicing in the beauty and warmth of love and the banishment of barren, cold hearts. Man must have his mate and his home; otherwise, "what were man?—a world without a sun!" (l. 24). In this part there are echoes from Milton—*Paradise Lost*, "L'Allegro," and "Il Penseroso." Lines 25–38 describe man in the Garden of Eden, joyless "till woman smiled!" Then comes a philosophical paragraph that likely reflects Campbell's own experience with young love:

> True, the sad power to generous hearts may bring
> Delirious anguish on his fiery wing,—
> Barred from delight by Fate's untimely hand,
> By wealthless lot, or pitiless command;
> Or doomed to gaze on beauties that adorn
> The smile of triumph or the frown of scorn;
> While Memory watches o'er the sad review,
> Of joys that faded like the morning dew.
> Peace may depart; and life and nature seem
> A barren path, a wildness, and a dream! (ll. 39–48)

Still "Hope's creative spirit" comes to the aid of the unfortunate lover. As once an artist who desired to depict the beauty of Venus observed the charms of all the forms and faces of mortal beauties and combined them, "So thy fair hand, enamoured Fancy! gleans / The treasured pictures of a thousand scenes" (ll. 85–86). A loving husband's moods echo the theme of "L'Allegro" and "Il Penseroso" with the lover dreaming of happiness in his ideal habitats in both summer and winter. In the summer he enjoys the outdoors; in winter, snug in his cottage, he delights in reading Falconer's *Shipwreck,* Schiller's *The Robbers,* "the gentler melodies," or "Truth's historic page"—the wars of Julius Caesar or the murderous winter marches of Sweden's Charles XII.

The next section, lines 189–212, did not appear in the first edition. It contains an apostrophe to Imagination, accompanied by Hope, showing man seeking to know the origins of the universe. The contorted syntax obscures the meaning—that in the future man can hope to see all things that now he can perceive only through the imagination.

Hope, despite her role as a Siren on occasion, is loved still in old age even though Wisdom has proved her false, just as David, remembering better days, mourned for Absalom. "Unfading Hope" in the face of death conveys "the morning dream of life's eternal day" (l. 242).

Lines 245–374 were also added after the first edition. In them, Hope is apostrophized as the "Daughter of Faith" who can dispel all doubts about the unknown after death.

> Soul of the just! companion of the dead!
> Where is thy home, and whither art thou fled?
> Back to its heavenly source thy being goes,

Swift as the comet wheels to whence he rose;
Doomed on his airy path awhile to burn,
And doomed, like thee, to travel, and return (ll. 277–282).

These lines, published shortly before Wordsworth wrote his famous "Ode: Intimations of Immortality from Recollections of Early Childhood," may have influenced Wordsworth's "Whither is fled the visionary gleam? / Where is it now, the glory and the dream?" (ll. 57–58). The joy of remembering, the contrast between youth and age, and the hope in immortality are other resemblances between the two poems. Although Wordsworth was very critical of Campbell and of "The Pleasures of Hope," he did own a copy of the poem, and it is certainly possible that Campbell's materials were in the background of his own. Of course, Vaughan's "The Retreat" and, still further back, Plato's dialogues were their common sources.

Lines 295–358 condemn the skeptics "Who, mouldering earthward, 'reft of every trust, / In joyless union wedded to the dust" (ll. 299–300), would glorify frail man and see nothing beyond this life. Are all the discoveries of "star-eyed Science" only "to waft us home the message of despair?" (l. 326). "I smile on death," says the poet, "if heavenward Hope remain!" (l. 334). Life is more than Chance. "Doubt, the mother of Dismay" (l. 359) can "pause at her martyr's tomb" (l. 360), the grave of a suicide called "poor lost Alonzo."

Though joys cease, says the poet, "the light of Hope," even hopeless hope or hope without reality, must remain. "What though my wingèd hours of bliss have been, / Like angel-visits, few and far between?" (ll. 377–78). Love, Beauty, and many of life's pleasures are transient, but eternal Hope consoles: "Congenial spirits part to meet again!" (l. 406). The following episode, that of Conrad and Ellenore, shows Conrad, "the martyr of his crimes," now "doomed the long isles of Sydney Cove to see" (ll. 411–12), bidding his daughter Ellenore a tearful, sentimental farewell, reassuring her of reunion "beyond the realms of Nature and of Time!" (l. 420).

Memory itself, Campbell feels, is an assurance of immortality:

If in that frame no deathless spirit dwell,
If that faint murmur be the last farewell,
If fate unite the faithful but to part,
Why is their memory sacred to the heart?
Why does the brother of my childhood seem
Restored awhile in every pleasing dream? (ll. 459–64)

(Here he is alluding to his brother James, who drowned at the age of thirteen while bathing in the river Clyde.)

Hope, present from the beginning of time, will survive the last man and the dissolution of the universe, and will, "undismayed, . . . o'er the ruin smile, / And light . . . [her] torch at Nature's funeral pile!" (ll. 473–74). The young Campbell had enunciated his theory of the importance of hope as a pleasure in itself. Keeping that torch alight was essential to him in both his life and his career.

Immediately after its publication, "The Pleasures of Hope" attracted critical notice. The *Analytical Review* praised it in June 1799,[1] with reservations: "The poetry of this little volume, if it do not exhibit marks of extraordinary genius, is yet by no means contemptible. It displays a fancy of considerable activity at least, if not vigour; a mind well cultivated, if not philosophical; and sentiments of the most ardent zeal in the cause of liberty" (p. 622). After a short summary with quotations from the poem, the reviewer judges: "Perhaps but a small portion of it can be allowed to be descriptive of the *pleasures of hope*. The second part, which we think inferior to the first, describes rather the pleasures of *sympathy*" (p. 623).

The *British Critic*, Tory and High Church, devoted six pages to it in July 1799, lauding the young poet's achievement but criticizing his libertarian principles, which the writer hoped "maturer age will correct."[2] The topic, "surely as good a subject for a rising poet, as can well be chosen," is treated "with much genius" and "with a very singular splendour and felicity of versification." The appeal of the poem is in its forming "ideal scenes of future gratification; which, if not at all destined to be realized, confer, for the time, an actual happiness by anticipation; and thus snatch from fate even more than it designs to give" (p. 21). This reviewer likewise accurately terms the first part superior to the second in clearness of style and transitions. "We should conceive the second part to be an after-thought. Perceiving that he had omitted the most material object of Hope, the hope of a future life, the author wrote perhaps the second part for the sake of leading the reader to it. But he bestowed less care, and exercised less judgment in performing this second task; possibly from weariness, possibly from a pardonable, though injudicious impatience, to lay the composition before the public" (pp. 21–22). Part II "is affected, and tainted with false refinement, in the thoughts, as well as many expressions" (p. 26). The reviewer intends "not to injure the Poem, which we admire, but to put the author on his guard when he shall correct it." He urges the poet to "cultivate his great talent for poetry" but "on no account, to omit that strict and severe criticism on himself, which alone can keep his genius within the limits of correct taste" (p. 26). Lack of clarity, inadequate transitions, obscure allusions, "weak or dubious expressions," verses whose "application to the subject" is "not sufficiently marked" are faults Campbell's critics have noticed ever since. Dr. Anderson's efforts in encouraging Campbell to revise the work obviously succeeded better in Part I than in Part II.

According to Cyrus Redding, some readers thought Campbell composed the poem in sections and then arranged them later, possibly intending the present opening lines for the conclusion.[3] A manuscript now in the British Museum, supposedly the first draft of the poem, is accompanied by an unsigned letter saying that it was first written in portions separately entitled, such as "The Sailor" and "The Emigrant," and that Campbell wove them together at Dr. Anderson's suggestion.

An early notice in the *Monthly Review*, written by Alexander Hamilton, a Sanscrit scholar-professor, also comments on Campbell's difficulty in providing "natural transitions" and his failure to adopt a "settled mode of arrangement . . . in disposing of the successive pictures which constitute the poem."[4] The work lacks "incident" and has "no story to embellish it" (p. 426). Its "characteristic style . . . is *the pathetic*, though in some passages it rises into a higher tone" (p. 422). The rather conservative Hamilton, noting that "in all his allusions to politics, Mr. Campbell takes no notice of the French Revolution," hopes that Campbell's mind is not tinged "with improper principles" and that the poet does disapprove of the "horrors and excesses" in France (p. 424). Contrary to other critics, Hamilton judges Part II "still more pleasing" than Part I: in the passages on immortality "the poem rises into a tone of unvaried sublimity, suited to the sacred nature of the subject" (p. 426). The conclusion he especially likes. Despite its defects, the poem is "entitled to rank among the productions of our superior Bards of the present day, as it unquestionably contains many striking proofs of the juvenile author's capacity for genuine and sublime poetry" (p. 426).

Other poets in Campbell's day commented later on "The Pleasures of Hope." Samuel Rogers, whose "Pleasures of Memory" helped inspire Campbell, said Campbell's poem was "no great favorite" with him. Rogers reported the opinion of Wordsworth, whose own poems were catching on more slowly than Campbell's: "Campbell's *Pleasures of Hope* has been strangely overrated: its fine words and sounding lines please the generality of readers, who never stop to ask themselves the meaning of a passage." Lines 58–60 of Part I to Wordsworth were "sheer nonsense,—nothing more than a poetical indigestion."[5] In his *Diary* Henry Crabb Robinson recorded Wordsworth's criticisms of Campbell's discordant imagery in this passage.[6]

Coleridge's opinion was equally unfavorable. According to the diary of John Payne Collier, November 1, 1811, Coleridge stated that Campbell, along with Scott and Southey, would not "by their poetry survive much beyond the day when they lived and wrote. Their works seemed to him not to have the seeds of vitality, the real germs of long life." Campbell,

in his "Pleasures of Hope" obviously had no fixed design, but when a thought (of course, not a very original one) came into his head, he put it down in couplets, and afterwards strung the *disjecta membra* (not *poetae*) together. Some of the best things in it were borrowed: for instance, the line—"And Freedom shriek'd when Kosciusko fell" was taken from a much ridiculed piece by Dennis, a Pindaric on William III.—"Fair Liberty shriek'd out aloud, aloud Religion groaned." . . . Coleridge had little toleration for Campbell, and considered him, as far as he had gone, a mere verse-maker.[7]

Scott, a friend and admirer of Campbell, told Thomas Moore, who was visiting him, that he considered "The Pleasures of Hope" "very inferior" to Campbell's "lesser pieces" like "Hohenlinden."[8] Byron, on the other hand, wrote in "English Bards and Scotch Reviewers": "Come forth, oh Campbell! give thy talents scope; / Who dares aspire if thou must cease to hope?" In a footnote, he called "The Pleasures of Hope," along with Rogers' "The Pleasures of Memory," "the most · beautiful didactic poems in our language, if we except Pope's *Essay on Man.*"[9]

The prose writers also had their say. Hazlitt in his *Lectures on the English Poets* charged that in "The Pleasures of Hope," "a painful attention is paid to the expression in proportion as there is little to express, and the decomposition of prose is substituted for the composition of poetry. . . . The sense and keeping in the ideas are sacrificed to a jingle of words and epigrammatic turn of expression." He annoyed Campbell by accusing him of borrowing the famous line "Like angel-visits, few and far between" from Blair's "Grave": "Its visits, / Like those of angels, short, and far between"—and then spoiling the expression by altering it. " 'Few', and 'far between,' are the same thing."[10] In his "Critical List of Authors" for *Select British*

Poets, Hazlitt said "The Pleasures of Hope" is "too artificial and antithetical."[11]

Hunt chose Campbell for number three in his *Sketches of the Living Poets,* commenting as follows on "The Pleasures of Hope":

There was an inauspicious look in the title of his first production. . . . It seemed written not only because Mr. Rogers's *Pleasures of Memory* had been welcomed into the critical circles, but because it was the next thing to writing a prose theme upon the *Utility of Expectation.* A youth might have been seduced into this by the force of imitation; but on reading the poem, it is impossible not to be struck with the willing union of the author's genius and his rhetoric. When we took it up the other day, we had not read it for many years, and found we had done it injustice; but the rhetoric keeps a perverse pace with the poetry.

He continues, observing Campbell's style and prosody:

The writer is eternally balancing his sentences, rounding his periods, epigrammatizing his paragraphs; and yet all the while he exhibits so much imagination and sensibility that one longs to have rescued his too delicate wings from the clippings and stintings of the school, and set him free to wander about the universe. Rhyme, with him, becomes a real chain. He gives the finest glances about him, and afar off, like a bird, spreads his pinions as if to sweep to his object; and is pulled back by his string into a chirp and a flutter. He always seems daunted and anxious. His versification is of the most received fashion; his boldest imaginings recoil into the coldest and most customary personifications. If he could have given up his pretty finishing commonplaces, his sensibility would sometimes have wanted nothing of vigour as well as tenderness.

We should not have said so much of this early poem, had the line been more strongly marked between the powers that produced it, and those of his later ones.[12]

Despite the criticisms, Professor William E. Aytoun stated in the 1850s that "The Pleasures of Hope" had maintained and even increased its popularity and was still "a universal favorite." "It is not too much to say," he added, "that it is, without any exception, the finest didactic poem in the English language."[13]

Today's readers would hardly agree with such high praise, but the poem's contemporary popularity can be judged by the fact that Mundell and Son of Edinburgh, the original publishers in April 1799, printed a ninth edition in 1806. In a period of hope and belief in human improvement and the age of the Godwinian doctrine of perfectibility, it caught the prevailing mood of idealism that included the glorification of home and moral values. Campbell voiced his own aspirations, in opposition to the fatalism of some of his countrymen. He dealt with topics already in the minds of his readers, such as freedom from oppression and interest in travel, and they responded gratefully to a relevant work that said "What oft was thought, but ne'er so well expressed."[14] Contradictions, borrowings, and poetic defects did not deter the common reader.

The reception of the poem inspired musicians, who set parts of it to music—particularly the destruction of Warsaw and the fall of Kosciusko; artists, who illustrated it with woodcuts to reveal "to the eye what the verse has addressed to the understanding and the heart," so that "we see as well as feel";[15] and translators, who made it available to French and German readers. Numerous American editions attest to its favorable reception across the Atlantic.

J. C. Hadden, one of Campbell's biographers, sourly observed in his discussion of the poem that "in literature popularity bears no strict proportion to merit. . . . Given certain vulgar ideas, the power of fluent and forcible expression, and no great depth of thought or sublety of imagination, and the breath of popular applause may generally be counted upon." He did concede, however, that "the poem was at least a credit to his years" and that its popularity can be accounted for mainly from its "vigour, variety, pleasant description, sincere rhetoric, youthful fervour and high spirits."[16]

Except for a few passages, "The Pleasures of Hope" holds little interest for modern readers. To sit down and read it through requires great patience and poetic faith. Nevertheless, in its unevenness, it does contain gems of pure poetry, showing Campbell as a true artist in his use of sound effects and pictorial vividness. In the judgment of Peter S. Macaulay, "Much of the *Pleasures of Hope* is verbose and turgid, but in his true poetic moments his style is economical at the same time that it is suggestive. . . . Within the *Pleasures of Hope* itself, there is a considerable range of styles and poetic techniques, this variety being emphasized by the skilful use of contrast."[17] Macaulay observes that "few lines are more delicately beautiful" and "further from mere rural elegance" than lines 99–102 of Part II:

> And when the sun's last splendour lights the deep,
> The woods and waves, and murmuring winds asleep;
> When fairy harps the Hesperian planet hail,
> And the lone cuckoo sighs along the vale . . . .

"The last line," he says, "is quintessentially romantic."[18]

Over the years, "The Pleasures of Hope" has been widely quoted and anthologized. Today it still belongs in anthologies of the Romantic period, with modern editors carefully choosing those passages that best represent what the poem meant to its contemporary readers as well as those lines that have a timeless appeal.

II "Gertrude of Wyoming; or, The Pennsylvanian Cottage"

Campbell's own favorite long poem was "Gertrude of Wyoming." During the time he was writing it, he declared himself to be " 'in high love with the work' " (Beattie, 1:499). The inspiration for the narrative poem, a domestic tragedy told in the idealized setting of a pastoral romance, came from several sources: Campbell's reading (the German novel *Barneck und Saldorf* by Lafontaine, published in 1804, the French novel *Atala* by Chateaubriand, 1801, and Thomson's poem "The Castle of Indolence," 1748); his own *Annals of Great Britain*, which contains a passage on the massacre that occurred at Wyoming, Pennsylvania, in 1778; his sympathy with the American Revolution and his thwarted desires to visit the United States and perhaps settle there himself; his happy marriage and family situation at the time (note Part I, stanzas 11 and 12, depicting a joyful parent-child relationship); and an expansion of the themes of freedom, human nobility, and love that he had used in "The Pleasures of Hope." On May 3, 1808, Campbell wrote to his friend John Richardson, requesting Richardson to send him a copy of Saint Pierre's *Paul and Virginia* in English. This sentimental tragedy about two children of nature in an idyllic setting, which Campbell read while he was writing "Gertrude," must also have had an influence on the poem. The fact that Scott had recently scored successes with two of his long poetic romances, "The Lay of the Last Minstrel" (1805) and "Marmion" (1808), and was to bring out "The Lady of the Lake" in 1810 could have encouraged Campbell to try the same genre.

The setting of Campbell's poem, the beautiful Wyoming valley of the Susquehanna River in eastern Pennsylvania, is sublime, a settler's dream where, contrary to history, love and brotherhood are undisturbed by anything more than memories from the past or stories from afar of "warring Europe." "Distance lends enchantment to the view,"[19] and Campbell idealizes not only the setting but also the characters. Gertrude, the heroine, possesses the beauty and virtues of a Miranda reared in isolated innocence; Albert, her widowed patriarchal father, has the wisdom and compassion of Prospero and Gonzalo; Henry Waldegrave, the Ferdinand of the story, epitomizes the romantic hero; and Outalissi, the Oneyda Indian chief, is a noble savage with none of the bestiality of Caliban. The theme is freedom violated by evil in the person of "the Monster" Brandt, the Mohawk Indian who demonstrates "what man has made of man,"[20] like the traitorous Sebastian and Antonio who betray their brothers in *The Tempest*.

The sentiment, the pathos, and the hope in immortality found in "The Pleasures of Hope" are all here; Campbell is definitely writing *con amore*. In the poem, he combines his classicism and interest in the Golden Age with the contemporary Romantic movement and its interest in primitivism. For instance, he expresses the same idea of the beneficent influence of nature that Wordsworth used in "Lines Written in Early Spring":

> It seem'd as if those scenes sweet influence had
> On Gertrude's soul, and kindness like their own
> Inspired those eyes affectionate and glad,
> That seem'd to love what'er they look'd upon (II.4).

Wordsworth's "Ruth" could have been another influence, for Ruth, like Gertrude, is "an infant of the woods."[21] Actually, the whole pastoral tradition is in the background. Immediate models for Albert and Gertrude were Campbell's Sydenham neighbors, Wynell Mayow and his daughter Mary.

For his medium Campbell chose the Spenserian stanza, used by Spenser in *The Faerie Queene* to describe similar idealized settings disturbed by the evils man perpetrates on man and more recently used by Thomson for his enchanted landscape in "The Castle of Indolence." Unlike the epigrammatic "Pleasures of Hope," "Gertrude of Wyoming" contains few detachable quotations.

The eighty-seven stanzas of the poem are logically divided into three parts, focused on Gertrude's childhood, marriage, and death. Into each part comes an invader of her paradise. The first, when she is nine years old, is Outalissi, who brings the boy Henry Waldegrave, orphaned in an attack by the Huron Indians on an English frontier fort, to Albert, an old friend of the Waldegraves. Part I concludes with Outalissi's "song of parting to the boy" (st 24), his "own adopted one" (st. 26), and his departure "with bark and plumage bright" (st. 28).

The second invader is the grown up Henry Waldegrave, who in Iberian boots and Spanish plume comes upon Gertrude, now a beautiful young woman, in the "deep untrodden grot" (II. 9), where "with Shakespeare's self she speaks and smiles alone" (II. 11). He seeks Albert's home, where he is welcomed without revealing his identity. There he tells the tales of his adventures, and Albert responds with the story of young Waldegrave, whose kinfolk in England, we now learn, had sent for him when he was twelve. At that dramatic moment, Gertrude recognizes him, and he explains that his Spanish disguise was donned as protection against possible disappointment and grief.

In Part III, after only "three little moons" of the fulfilled dream of love for Henry and Gertrude, the American Revolution portends "a husband to the battle doom'd to go" (st. 8). Suddenly, late one night, Outalissi bursts into their bower. Although he is aged by "fifteen years' despair," Henry still recognizes him, and a sentimental reunion ensues. Despite his sad condition, he is able after a time to warn his friends of the imminent threat of Brandt's forces, who have already destroyed all of his kindred. The settlers flee to the neighboring fort, where Albert falls from an Indian arrow and dies in the arms of Gertrude. She, presumably wounded also, then dies in the arms of Henry, first assuring him of eternal love. The poem ends with Outalissi's consolation and death song.

Campbell's decision to use the Spenserian stanza caused him problems. The limitations of the rhyme scheme resulted in contorted sentences, such as "Then, where of Indian hills the daylight takes / His leave, how might you the flamingo see / Disporting like a meteor on the lakes" (I. 3). (Campbell failed to research his natural history when he assigned tropical flamingos and crocodiles to Pennsylvania.) Other obvious faults are manipulation of plot—having Outalissi return as a *deus ex machina* to warn his white friends of the imminent Indian attack; *ex post facto* explanation—having Waldegrave evidently disappear after Part I and reappear incognito in Part II as a well-traveled young Aeneas ripe for marriage; and vague narration—at the end of Part II, having Henry and Gertrude fall in love and marry, with the situation beautifully obscured for the reader's imagination to complete. Finally, killing off father and daughter as chance targets of an Indian arrow or arrows produces only pathos, not true tragedy.

In creating the character Brandt, Campbell says in his notes to the poem that he used "the common Histories of England, all of which represented him as a bloody and bad man (even among savages), and chief agent in the horrible desolation of Wyoming" (p. 91). In 1821, much to his surprise, Brandt's son, a young Mohawk Indian chief, visited Campbell in England and asked that he retract the defamation of his father's character. The son had with him documents that proved not only that his father, Captain Joseph Brant, "was not even present at that scene of desolation," but that "he often strove to mitigate the cruelty of Indian warfare" (p. 92). In these notes to subsequent editions, different from those of the first edition, Campbell expresses his regret and states: "The name of Brandt, therefore, remains in my poem a pure and declared character of fiction" (p. 92). He did not reconstruct the poem to change the name Brandt, however.

In the notes, Campbell also alludes to an article he placed in the *New Monthly Magazine* in 1822 entitled "Letter to the Mohawk Chief Ahyonwaeghs, Commonly Called John Brant, Esq. of the Grand River, Upper Canada, from Thomas Campbell." (A footnote explains that the correct spelling of the name is Brant.) In the "Letter" he comments: "I really knew not, when I wrote my poem, that the son and daughter of an Indian chief were ever likely to peruse it, or be affected by its contents." (Neither had Campbell known that after 1783, Joseph Brant had also visited England, where he was honored for his service to England during the Revolution.) Campbell explains his sources, apologizes to the younger Brant, and clarifies his father's friendship with the British. In the article, Campbell also answers the accusations of some of his reviewers that he was unpatriotic. He defends the American cause, saying that "the American war was disgraceful only to those who were its abettors, and . . . the honor of Englishmen is redeemed in proportion as they deprecate its principles and deplore its details." A poet, he maintains, may be the *"moral censor"* of his country, *"and he must not be her parasite."*[22] A later historical work, *Border Wars of the American Revolution,* corroborates John Brant's testimony, terms Campbell's "Letter" "less magnanimous, and characterized by more of special pleading, than might have been expected," and regrets that the wrong was not fully redressed by "one of the most gifted bards of the age" in the text of the next edition of his poem, instead of merely in a note.[23]

Campbell sent proof sheets of "Gertrude" to his friend Archibald Alison in Edinburgh, and he in turn showed them to Francis Jeffrey, editor of the Whiggish *Edinburgh Review.* Jeffrey responded with a letter to Campbell, dated March 1, 1809: "I have seen your Gertrude. . . . There is great beauty, and great tenderness, and fancy in the work—and I am sure it will be very popular." He liked the exquisite pathos of the latter part and the "purity and truth" of the whole, but he offered several criticisms: "In the first place, it is too short—not merely for the delight of the reader—but, in some degree, for the development of the story, and for giving full effect to the fine scenes that are delineated. It looks almost as if you had cut out large portions of it, and filled up the gaps very imperfectly." He criticized the missing links in the love story, the abrupt ending, and the faults in diction: "There is still a good deal of obscurity in many passages—and in others a strained and unnatural expression—an appearance of labor and hardness; you have hammered the metal in some places till it has lost all its ductility."

Wishing Campbell had had "courage to correct, or rather to avoid" his "faults of over-finishing," Jeffrey continued in a vein other critics afterwards mined: "I have another fault to charge you with in private—for which I am more angry with you than for all the rest. Your timidity, or fastidiousness, or some other knavish quality, will not let you give your conceptions glowing, and bold, and powerful, as they present themselves; but you must chasten, and refine, and soften them, forsooth, till half their nature and grandeur is chiselled away from them."

He urged the poet to "venture to cast before . . . [the world] some of the rough pearls" of his fancy, or if he wished, first to try one or two such poems on him. "I am more mistaken in my prognostics than I ever was in my life, if they are not twice as tall as any of your full-dressed children" (Beattie, 1:513-14).

On the same day that the poem appeared, in April 1809, the *Edinburgh Review* came out with a review of "Gertrude of Wyoming" as its leading article, written anonymously by Jeffrey.[24] He contrasted the poem favorably with other recent poetry, predicting that "Gertrude" and Campbell's other poems in the volume would outlast it as truer poetry. In "softness and beauty," "pathos and interest," "Gertrude" to him also outranked "The Pleasures of Hope" (p. 4). After praising "the pure and tender enchantment" (p. 6) of the new poem with extensive quotations, Jeffrey criticized it in much the same manner as in the letter. He hoped that for the sake of perspicuity, the poet would make additions in a new edition. Concluding that Campbell has "still greater promise than performance," he wished that he had "the power to give him confidence in his own great talents" (p. 19).

Also in April, the *Scots Magazine* reviewed "Gertrude."[25] That anonymous reviewer, considering Campbell's genius better at handling generalities than at depicting minute particulars, thought "The Pleasures of Hope" a better poem than "Gertrude of Wyoming." "Domestic pathos" and private sorrows do not befit the poet's talents. The best part of the poem, to this writer, is "that descriptive of Indian character, and Indian warfare" (p. 281). The rest rarely rises above mediocrity. He also pointed out that Campbell fails frequently to strengthen the final Alexandrine of his Spenserian stanzas, but does here refrain from converting "nouns and verbs into each other," which is a "strained use of language" found often in "The Pleasures of Hope" (p. 284).

The next month, the *Edinburgh's* new Tory rival, the *Quarterly Review*, in only its second number, published as its lead article a review of "Gertrude."[26] John Murray, founder of the *Quarterly* and a friend of Campbell, requested Walter Scott, also Campbell's friend despite political differences, to write the review anonymously. Scott, beginning "with no ordinary impression of the delicacy and importance of the task" (p. 241), felt the new work had to be judged in relation to Campbell's other poems and reputation. The beauties of "The Pleasures of Hope" had delighted many readers, who excused "the marks of a juvenile composition" and made allowances for "the didactic nature of the subject" that presented "in some degree the appearance of an unfinished picture" (pp. 241–42). Now, ten years later, "the hope of improvement," "the actual excellence of his first poem" (p. 242), and the success of some of the more recent shorter poems have combined to build high expectations for Campbell's new work, which was known to be underway for some time before it appeared. As could be expected in such a situation, said Scott, the fulfillment does not live up to the anticipation. While the poem has "passages both of tenderness and sublimity, which may decline comparison with few in the English language" (p. 243), it has several faults.

First, Scott expressed "a hope that Mr. Campbell will in his subsequent poems chuse [*sic*] a theme more honourable to our national character, than one in which Britain was disgraced by the atrocities of her pretended adherents. We do not love to have our feelings unnecessarily put in arms against the cause of our country" (p. 243). A poet, who, unlike a historian, can choose his materials, does not have to dishonor his own land, Scott felt.

"The great defect of the story" (p. 247) is the disappearance of Waldegrave, which causes the reader to lose "the thread of the story"

(p. 248) and to question the plausibility of a spontaneous love upon his return. Other smaller defects, such as unexplained motivations and improbabilities, are evident at the first reading, "whereas, after repeated perusals, we perceive beauties which had previously escaped our notice" (p. 254). According to his own artistic criteria, Scott wished Campbell had painted a larger canvas of the whole Wyoming massacre, instead of showing only the one family.

Scott disclaimed the customary superiority of the reviewer in perceiving the author; instead, he showed his understanding of the writing process. Noting that the first line of III.37—"To-morrow let us do or die!"—is found in Burns's "Bannockburn" ("Scots, Wha Hae"), he called it "a kind of common property, being the motto, we believe, of a Scottish family." He thus observed a truth that several of Campbell's later critics failed to heed: "But these occasional coinci-dences, over which stupidity delights to doze, are hardly worth noticing in criticizing original poetry" (p. 253n.).

Like Jeffrey, he pointed out that a writer can so revise and reconsider his work that he loses "the impulse of imagination" (p. 256). It is thus paradoxical that "the most obvious faults" in "Ger-trude" result from "the same cause which has undoubtedly produced many of the excellencies of the poem"—the author's "anxious and assiduous attention" to it (p. 254). In some passages, meaning is knit into a Gordian knot, and in others, "affected inversion" (p. 256) defaces the simple and natural. Scott indirectly accused Campbell of correcting the spirit out of the poem by following "the advice of literary friends" (p. 257).[27] In all, he did his duty with a sense of kindness, pointing out in his review the main criticisms he wrote in his letters about Campbell and to Campbell himself. Campbell was reportedly pleased with the review, but he did not know the identity of the author.

The *Monthly Review* noticed the poem in July, expressing disap-pointment with it and disgust with the "dictatorial cabal" (presuma-bly Jeffrey and his friends) attempting "to win the mass of readers." The reviewer, Thomas Denman, a lawyer, could see some re-semblances between "Gertrude" and James Beattie's "The Minstrel," which also used the Spenserian stanza. To him, the few excellent passages were lost amidst the preponderance of bad ones. He thought the only service that this poem could render its author's reputation was "lightening for the future that load of public expecta-tion, under which his poetical spirit appears to have sunken."[28]

The *London Review*, a close rival of the *Edinburgh*, devoted thirty-five pages to the "irksome and painful task" of examining "Gertrude" and contrasting it with Campbell's other poems.[29] The reviewer, Horace Twiss, a lawyer and politician, termed "Gertrude" a failure "forced into some kind of reputation, by a party, important alike from their literary talents and their social influence" (p. 46). Noting that this party admired the poem's "air of classical regularity which pervades the style, and characterizes the general effect," he sarcastically observed: "Now if there could ever be a season peculiarly favourable to the production of a work written according to the good primitive models, that season was certainly the moment when Gertrude appeared; because, from the circumstances of the times, the critics were disposed to welcome any thing, not absolutely wretched, that came in the simple shape of the antient favourites" (p. 46). He judged that Campbell's immortality will rest on "The Pleasures of Hope" and the war poems.

In September, the *Antijacobin Review* also attacked "Jeffery's [*sic*] *northern lights,* which have vainly attempted to cast a meridian lustre on the muse of his countryman, and occasional coadjutor."[30] This anonymous reviewer, holding a middle course, could see some beauties in the poem, but he was disappointed in it. Writing for a superpatriotic journal, he, like Scott, condemned Campbell's ascribing "the American rebellion" to "the oppression of the mother country." "This democratic whine is beneath his muse" (pp. 5–6). To him, a writer has an obligation: "An interesting poem, and an amusing novel, are the best channels of instruction to the general class of readers; and he who, having the ability to inform or amend others, neglects to employ it for that purpose, does not perform his duty to society" (p. 5). Campbell "seems chiefly anxious to sound the praises of *rebellion;* and to render rebels objects of interest and attachment" (p. 5). He should use better judgment, "quit affectation, and court simplicity" (p. 9).

The reviewer for the *British Critic* in October rejoiced that Campbell had heeded his advice given earlier about "The Pleasures of Hope" to exercise self-criticism, but now he felt the poet had overdone it.[31] Feeling partly responsible for the outcome, the reviewer-preceptor preferred at the present to "exult in the vigour and harmony which result" rather than "reprove a fault" (p. 368). However, he was sorry that Campbell did not take his political advice and choose a subject friendly to "the fair fame of his country" (p. 368). The great fault of a poem "American rather than English" is that Waldegrave evidently renounces everything in England and returns to America "to support what he falsely calls liberty" (p. 369). Still, Campbell is "a real poet" who ranks "among the best and most classical writers of the present day" (p. 372).

Most people discussing literature at all during this period had something to say about "Gertrude of Wyoming." Hazlitt, in his *Lectures on the English Poets* in 1818, termed "Gertrude" Campbell's "principal performance," but "a kind of historical para- phrase of Mr. Wordsworth's poem of Ruth." He named over the usually mentioned faults of the work and pointed out its "mechanical structure." "The most striking events occur in the shape of antith- eses. The story is cut into the form of a parallelogram. There is the same systematic alternation of good and evil, of violence and repose, that there is of light and shade in a picture."[32] In his *Select British Poets* in 1824, he was kinder, saying the poem "strikes at the heart of nature, and has passages of extreme interest."[33] The next year, in *The Spirit of the Age*, he judged that Campbell had "succeeded in engrafting the wild and more expansive interest of the romantic school of poetry on classic elegance and precision."[34]

To Leigh Hunt in 1821, "Gertrude of Wyoming," a "higher thing" than "The Pleasures of Hope," "has stuff in it that should have made it still better." Even with its faults, however, he had always loved "Gertrude." To him, Campbell "certainly has the faculties of a real poet; and it is not the fault of the *poets* of his country that he has not become a greater."[35]

Coleridge admitted that "Gertrude" "contained very pretty stan- zas."[36] Other writers were less impressed. John Keats and Dorothy Wordsworth disparaged the poem in their letters. Samuel Rogers liked its beautiful feeling and an occasional exquisite line but deplored some of its passages.[37] Robert Southey admitted that the poem was better than he had expected, "except in story, which is meagre." He believed Campbell had borrowed from Wordsworth's "The Brothers" as well as from "Ruth."[38]

Mrs. Anne Grant, a Scottish miscellaneous writer and critic, stated in one of her letters: "I admire and delight in Campbell," but she felt that the *Edinburgh Review's* "lavish eulogium" of "Gertrude of Wyoming" was overdone. In another letter she termed Campbell's "democratic hoof," which protrudes itself through the poem, "very provoking." Still, regardless of her annoyances and the faults of the piece, she saw and felt "all the charms of this exquisite poem."[39]

With the reviewers finding at least something good to say about the poem, the less critical public could be expected to respond favorably, and they did. Influenced by Jeffrey, the Whigs especially liked it. Three British editions were sold within two years, besides the American edition. The market was right for stories of domestic love and fidelity, and a narrative poem with romantic characters living in the exciting New World of opportunity was bound to be popular.

The first well-known poetic work in the English language set in North America and using an Indian as a character, "Gertrude of Wyoming" found a very favorable reception in the United States. Washington Irving, pointing out that Campbell is "the only British poet of eminence that has laid the story of a considerable poem, in the bosom of our country," confessed that "we were both surprised and gratified to meet with a poet, sufficiently unprejudiced to conceive an idea of moral excellence and natural beauty on this side of the Atlantic."[40] He felt that it was certainly to the interest of both countries for writers to help erase hostilities. "The writers of Great Britain are the adopted citizens of our country," who "exercise an authority over our opinions and affections, cherished by long habit and matured by affection" (p. 245).

Irving felt that in "Gertrude," Campbell had hallowed and immortalized a romantic locale in the infant nation, helping to remedy a "deficiency in those local associations produced by history and moral fiction" that consitute "a great source of national pride and love of country." Now Campbell's poem "may assist to convince many, who were before slow to believe, that our own country is capable of inspiring the highest poetic feelings" (p. 247).

Other American writers likewise appreciated "Gertrude of Wyoming." Robert C. Sands, magazine editor and miscellaneous writer from New York City, in an article on "Domestic Literature" referred to the work as "the sweetest of modern poems" in which "the ideals of the Indian character have been drawn . . . in the character of Outalissi, and exhibited in poetry as chaste as it is noble, as mellifluous as it is graphic."[41] Two early American poets alluded to Campbell in their poems on the Wyoming valley: Fitz-Greene Halleck in "Wyoming" (1821) and Mrs. Lydia H. Sigourney in "Zinzendorff" (1836). Oliver Wendell Holmes wrote that once when he crossed the Susquehanna River, he felt that his heart renewed "its allegiance to the poet who has made it lovely to the imagination as well as to the eye, and so identified his fame with the noble stream that it 'rolls mingling with his fame forever.' "[42]

On the whole, all of Campbell's poems, but especially "Gertrude of Wyoming," were popular in the United States, and Campbell valued this American favor. On a number of occasions, he stated his love for America and wished that he had been able at least to visit the country, particularly the Wyoming valley. One settler in the Susquehanna Valley above Wyoming, Nathaniel P. Willis, on the occasion of a rumor that Campbell was coming for an American visit, wrote "America would rise up to Campbell. He has been the bard of freedom, generous and chivalric in all his strains; and, nation of merchants as we are, I am mistaken if the string he has most played is not the master-chord of our national character. The enthusiasm of no people on earth is so easily awoke, and Campbell is the poet of enthusiasm. The schoolboys have him by heart, and what lives upon their lips, will live and be beloved for ever."[43]

Willis was not a prophet, however. "Gertrude" is no longer popular; nor is it available in anthologies. If it were accessible, modern readers would find themselves unable to identify with the characters or to respond to the poem as anything more than quaint historical fiction. In 1899, Hadden judged it as "a third-rate poem containing a few first-rate lines. It is practically dead, and can never be called back to life."[44] His evaluation is still correct. "Gertrude of Wyoming" is now a period piece.

III "Theodric: A Domestic Tale"

After "Gertrude of Wyoming," Campbell did not bring out another long poem for fifteen years; then "Theodric" appeared. If "Gertrude" is dead now, "Theodric" is even more so. This sentimental "domestic tale" of five hundred seventy-seven lines written in heroic couplets is a romantic love tragedy set in Switzerland and England. Its hero Theodric, is an Austrian colonel beloved by a Swiss maiden and an English beauty, both equally devoted, equally high-minded, and equally selfless—epitomes of the angelic women so admired at the time. Theodric, the foreign intruder into the lives of both, inadvertently causes the deaths of both of them.

The poem opens with a good nature passage, a sunset over a vast Swiss mountain landscape where "Earth's features so harmoniously were link'd, / She seem'd one great glad form" (ll. 16–17). Then the focus narrows to proximity—a Gothic churchyard where "rose blossom'd by each rustic tomb"—and centers on the grave of a maiden who, the inscription says, died young and fair. The comrade of the poet-speaker becomes the omniscient storyteller to relate the romance of this mountain maid who " 'died of love that could not be return'd' " (l. 35).

She was, it seems, an idealistic young lady who dreamed of marrying a heroic being "of chivalric kind" (l.55). When her sixteen-year-old brother Udolph went off to fight for the Austrian Empire, he joined the corps of Theodric, a valiant leader whom he worshiped as a hero and for whom he distinguished himself as a soldier. His glowing letters home consequently identified her idol in real life and set fire in his "wondering sister's well-believing breast" (l. 95). Julia (for so Campbell finally reveals her name to be) obviously has her literary forebear in Malory's Elaine, the "Lily Maid of Astolat" who died for her love of Sir Launcelot; and she is related also to Desdemona, who came to love Othello from hearing his tales of military feats.

When Udolph was wounded in battle, Theodric took care of him like a brother and wrote letters to his family informing them of his progress, thereby increasing their appreciation of their son's commander. Udolph, after recovery, fought on until the peace came, "A curtain-drop between the acts of death,— / A check in frantic war's unfinish'd game" (ll. 129-30). Although grieved to leave his chief, he rejoiced to return home, and in the "gayest room" of the house he hung a picture of Theodric, whom Julia recognized from a dream she had had of him.

Meanwhile Theodric went to England as a tourist. A chance postponement of his departure enabled him to attend a jubilee celebrating the Treaty of Amiens. "But how our fates from unmomentous things / May rise, like rivers out of little springs!" (ll. 168–69). Among the multitudes turning out for the illuminations in London, Theodric spotted a beautiful young woman in an open carriage, the motto and arms of which he noted. Following that clue he found her, one who

> with affections warm, intense, refined,
> . . . mix'd such calm and holy strength of mind,
> That, like Heaven's image in the smiling brook,
> Celestial peace was pictured in her look (ll. 188-91).

In true storybook fashion "he won her—and resolved to make / His future home in England for her sake" (ll. 198–99).

Before the wedding, however, he was called back to Austria for "a season's space" (l. 202), and enroute he stopped off in Switzerland to visit Udolph and his family. Overjoyed, they would not permit a "speedy parting," and he, "loth to wound their hospitable pride" (l. 208), promised to stay with them for a month. Inevitably, "friendship grew" between Theodric and Julia. For Theodric it was only friendship, the narrator points out, because "he who had loved Constance could not change!" (l. 221). For Julia, though, it was otherwise.

When her emotions betrayed her, and Theodric came to realize her true feelings, he honorably told her of his betrothal to Constance. She took his answer gracefully; but when he later admitted that if he had come to Switzerland before going to England, things might have been different, she was overcome with grief and he with contrition. She consoled herself with what might have been: " 'To think I could have merited your faith / Shall be my solace even unto death!' " (ll 268–69). Although he abjured her by her " 'pure and sacred peace of mind, / And by the dignity of womankind' " (ll. 272–73) to swear to forget this love after his departure, she could not speak the vow. Then from her mother he learned that this affection was inevitable, nursed " 'like fatality,' " their hospitality bound to encourage it despite his blamelessness. He departed, and Julia, "lingering at her window, long survey'd / His boat's last glimpses melting into shade" (ll. 306–07).

From Austria, where he was relieved to hear from Udolph "that Julia's mind / Had borne his loss, firm, tranquil, and resign'd" (ll. 310–11), he returned to England to marry Constance, who is portrayed as a superlative example of "that mighty truth—how happy are the good!" (l. 325). Their home was "a little Heaven, above dissension's reach" (l. 333), but her family, "save one congenial sister" (l. 335) were the kind of in-laws one would least choose. They were "foils to her bright intellect and grace, / As if she had engross'd the virtue of her race" (ll. 336–37). Constance's role as family counselor and appeaser frequently caused her to be away from home, but Theodric "bore her absence for its pious end" (l. 343).

As the situation becomes complicated, Campbell's telling becomes obscure. "German honour" demanded Theodric's help in his native land, and Constance, saying " 'Your fame is mine' " (l. 352), urged him to let her accompany him despite the hazards. He overruled her, "And she express'd assent, although her heart / In secret had resolved they should not part" (ll. 358–59). Then the narrator moralizes: "How oft the wisest on misfortune's shelves / Are wreck'd by errors most unlike themselves!" (ll. 360–61). He mentions a "little fault," a "fraud of love's romance," a "plan's concealment," that "wrought their whole mischance" (ll. 362–63). She promised to write Theodric something that would make him happy, but failed "haplessly" to reveal her plan before going off again to her worthless kindred. He, lonely, and "damp'd in thoughts" (l. 732), began to think about the past and about Udolph, "And deep misgivings on his spirit fell / That all with Udolph's household was not well" (ll. 374–75). Again Campbell writes of premonition: " 'Twas that too true prophetic mood of fear / That augurs griefs inevitably near" (ll. 376–77).

Sure enough, Udolph, much changed, surprised him with a visit that morning, bringing news that Julia, who had tried to hide her grief, gave way to secret woe and has long pined, " 'for broken hearts die slow!' " (l. 389). Feeling the approach of death, she is now yearning to see Theodric once more. Udolph, blaming his " 'insane ambition for the name / Of brother to Theodric' " (ll. 397-98) for encouraging " 'those high-built hopes that crush'd her by their fall' " (l. 399), explained that he had made the long journey to seek one more visit by Theodric. He knew that Constance would have no " 'fear of a poor dying object's love' " (l. 407). Suddenly their conversation was interrupted by the intrusion of Constance's kindred, who took perverse pleasure in tormenting Theodric with the news that Constance would remain away for another fortnight. Theodric, vexed, "blamed his Constance's intent" (l. 420). When the kinsmen departed, however, they left him a note from Constance explaining all, saying she was remaining only to make a parting peace, and "pray'd for love to share his foreign life,/ And shun all future chance of kindred strife" (ll. 426-27). He wrote his consent, but "The letter miss'd her on her homeward way" (l. 429). Nevertheless, within six hours she was in his arms, upset by the news her kinsmen had brought her that he was angry. The reunion mingled pain and pleasure, pride and terror, "lest his few rash words mistold / Had agonised her pulse to fever's heat" (ll. 443-44). Soon Constance, calm, composed, and sympathetic with Julia, implored Theodric to attend "her dying wish" (l. 450) and accompany Udolph to see her while she awaited his return. " 'And then we'll cross the deep, and part no more' " (l. 453).

The next day, Theodric left with Udolph, feeling "a dark presenti-ment / Some ailment lurk'd, ev'n whilst she smiled, to mock / His fears of harm from yester-morning's shock" (ll. 459-61). They reached Switzerland with an appropriate tempest raging, and "the wolf's long howl in dismal discord join'd" (l. 471).[45] Julia "still knew him—smiled on him with feeble laugh— / And bless'd him, till she drew her latest sigh!" (ll. 477-78).

Amidst their grief, Theodric's second premonition came true. The faithful page he had left at home, alerted to notify him if any change occurred in Constance's health, appeared with the dramatic news that Constance "still was living" when he set out, "but whether now was left in doubt" (ll. 484-85). "In the human breast / Two master-passions cannot co-exist" (ll. 488-89), the narrator comments. Theodric, stunned, and fancying he saw Constance beneath Julia's shroud, hurried home, traveling day and night. Unlike Julia, however, Constance did not linger for his arrival. Her sister informed the suffering husband that the one to blame for his wife's death was their mother, who, for the family's sake, did not want her daughter to leave the land. Unable to change Constance's intentions, she "grew incensed" and so upset Constance that her ailment, till then "slight, or none," caused her to droop rapidly, "and fatal pains came on" (ll. 523–29).

Before her death, Constance had dictated and signed a letter to Theodric. Ironically, as Theodric had earlier done to Julia on departing from her, his wife was now conjuring him " 'to bear / . . . [her] loss with noble spirit—not despair' " (ll. 560-61), and in promise to kiss the letter where she had left her kiss. The maudlin ending finds him obtaining solace and harmony with life, as if her spirit watched over him.

This sentimental poem, its double catastrophe based on chance rather than character, appealed to audiences who liked to sympathize and weep. In it Campbell no doubt exorcised some of his personal sorrow and his increasing anxieties over the mental illness of his son, now institutionalized, and over his wife's failing health. Whether his hero, Theodric, for whom two ladies died, had any private meaning for him otherwise is a question.

After "Theodric" had been out a month, Campbell wrote to Richardson: " 'I am very glad that Jeffrey is going to review me; for I think *he* has the stuff in him to understand *Theodric*' " (Beattie, 2:163). Jeffrey's critique was the leading article in the *Edinburgh Review* for January 1825.[46] He began by laughing that Campbell "has even acquired, by virtue of his exemplary laziness, an assurance and pledge of immortality which he could scarcely have obtained without it" (p. 271). His "twenty years' intermission" (a five years' exaggeration) has tested and proved his immortality. "There is . . . no living poet . . . whose advertisement excites greater expectation than Mr. Campbell's:—and a new poem from him is waited for with even more eagerness (as it is certainly for a much longer time) than a new novel from the author of Waverley" (p. 271). Again, "high expectation . . . has its drawbacks and its dangers," for a popular author's worst rival is "his former self" (pp. 271-72). The public must not think, though, that infrequent publication means that a new poem has been incubating during all of the time lapsed since its predecessor. "Men of genius, whose thoughts play with the ease and rapidity of lightning, often seem tardy to the public, because there are long intervals between the flashes!" (p. 287).

Jeffrey's description of the poem makes it sound like a sentimental television serial:

It is entitled 'a Domestic Story,'—and it is so—turning upon few incidents—embracing few characters—dealing in no marvels and no terrors—displaying no stormy passions. Without complication of plot, in short, or hurry of action—with no atrocities to shudder at, or feats of noble daring to stir the spirits of the ambitious,—it passes quietly on, through the shaded paths of private life, conversing with gentle natures and patient sufferings—and unfolding, with serene pity and sober triumph, the pangs which are fated at times to wring the breast of innocence and generosity, and the courage and comfort which generosity and innocence can never fail to bestow (p. 272).

He complimented the poem's "taste and feeling," "fine and tender finish," "chastened elegance of words and images," "mild dignity and tempered pathos," and "general tone of simplicity and directness" (p. 272). Difficulties he found include "passages that are somewhat *fade*," "expressions that are trivial," and differences between the "two distinct compartments—one relating to the Swiss maiden, the other to the English wife" (p. 273). Especially in Constance's farewell letter, Campbell was guilty of "poverty of invention in the structure of his pathetic narratives" (p. 281). Jeffrey could see that the poet was still having his old problems: elucidation, motivation, and abruptness.

Jeffrey's friendly Whiggish puffery was more than his Tory rivals could take. The youthful writers of *Blackwood's Edinburgh Magazine* with great *jeu d'esprit* came out with an article entitled "The Bairnly School of Criticism, No. I, Leading Article (*On Theodric*) in the Edinburgh Review."[47] In it, they have Jeffrey as president of "the Bairnly Club," whose "aim and object is the promotion of gaiety and innocence (p. 486). One duty of the holder of this office is "to furnish the Leading Article to the Blue and Yellow" (the *Edinburgh Review*) (p. 486). Of the review of "Theodric," "the Bairnly Club are proud, and justly proud. . . . We conceive it to be by far the bairnliest critique of the year." They "call the public attention to a few of its most striking beauties," quoting the most extreme statements of "Francisculus" (p. 486). Then the rowdy bairns pay Jeffrey their highest compliment "by electing Tom Campbell an Honorary Member of the Bairnly Club" (p. 487).

In the same issue of *Blackwood's* appeared "MS. Notes on the last Number of the Edinburgh Review,"[48] commenting on Jeffrey's "exquisite drivel on Tom Campbell's already forgotten piece of imbecility—*the* Theodric" (p. 461). The writer chides Jeffrey's "really poor work" in "gravely clapping the trumpet to his lips, and blowing a Paean" for what "the whole world has decided . . . is a weak, silly, puerile, ineffective, unimaginative, unreadable screed of trash" (p. 461).

The official review of "Theodric" in *Blackwood's*[49] is a more serious and perceptive one, the reviewer concluding that "this poem, with all its tenderness and beauty, is now in the greatest jeopardy, and can only be saved by Mr Jeffrey from being damned. . . . Mr Campbell is his friend—and what is friendship without active offices?" (p. 108). After recalling the delights of reading the "beautiful" "Pleasures of Hope," in which "the untamed soul of youth spoke in every line" (p. 102), the writer, a mature critic who can now see the numerous faults of that poem, suggested that Campbell's fame will rest with the "vast crowd of young people in the world," most of whom "will admire and delight" in him. "Every promising youth will buy a copy of the Pleasures of Hope, in his fifteenth year, or sooner if precocious. Edition will pursue Edition: Campbell will always be a Classic—and elegantly bound and richly lettered, he will, as far as we can see, lie on the drawing-room tables of the ingenuous and polite, until the extinction of civility in this empire" (p. 102).

The reviewer was not "so greatly disappointed as all the rest of the reading world" with "Theodric," he said. It is "very, very pretty, very pathetic even; there is much that is Campbellish about it, and it cannot be said, fairly and candidly, that it does him absolute discredit. Yet, we did expect a better poem" (p. 104). He accused Campbell of "a barrenness, not of invention only, but absolutely of feeling" (p. 107). "The tale illustrates nothing that we can discern worth illustrating." The reader's sympathy "is never once excited during the whole poem; the heart of the reader is almost always pained, and his understanding dissatisfied" (p. 108).

Like Wordsworth, noted the reviewer, Campbell tried to use simple language, but unlike Wordsworth, whose simplicity is generally "sublime," Campbell, whose "genius is altogether of a different stamp . . . must have the air of elegance to breathe, or he gasps, chokes, and dies. In Theodric he often tries to be homely, familiar, conversationally narrative, to write as if in a newspaper of daily occurrences, marriages, births, and deaths. Then is he uniformly silly and conceited" (p. 108).

The pedantic Tory *Quarterly Review* answered Jeffrey's excuses for Campbell's small production of poetry:

To the real poet poetry is the vocation of his life; from every thing within and without him, the appearances of nature and the achievements of art, from study of books and meditation on himself, he is every day and every hour deriving fresh materials for his occupation, and additional skill in the use of them. The moment of composition is that of his greatest delight—it is not therefore to be expected that he should write either very slowly or seldom; and though it is a mistake to suppose that the labour of correction is [not?] cold or painful, still, as habit will tend to give his first conceptions clearness, and his first expressions fitness, and as a sense of his own power will give decision to his judgment, the necessity and the inclination to correct will gradually diminish.[50]

Like other critics, this one, the Reverend Edward Smedley, lamented Campbell's lack of maturation with time.[51] "Theodric" has, instead degraded the poet. The title character "is, in truth, no other than an involuntary Macheath" from Gay's "Beggar's Opera" (p. 346). The poem has no "redeeming beauties," and "all is tame and languid; we are left to gather the characters of the leading personages from vague generalities; to take the poet's word for what they are, not to learn it from our observation of themselves." He finds fault with the prosaic language, diction "vulgar without being simple," incorrect rhymes, and bad versification (pp. 347–48).

His conclusion is percipient: "There is, and has been for some time, a growing persuasion, slowly and reluctantly entertained by the public, (for Mr. Campbell has ever found in the public a favourable and faithful audience,) that the character of his mind is to be feeble and minute. Such a poem as Theodric must impart fearful strength to such an opinion. Yet we will struggle against the conviction; literary history is not without examples of failures great as this, and there may be circumstances of mind or body which may account for them." He urges Campbell to "withdraw from every avocation," and exert himself to regain "that respectable rank from which we are sincerely sorry that he has declined." Then "this unworthy publication" can be forgotten (pp. 348–49).

Other periodical writers were hard put to say something even moderately kind. The *British Critic* reluctantly lectured Campbell on a number of faults but stated that "the description of Udolph's first campaign is not merely good, but it possesses the merit of Mr. Campbell's other battle pieces, both naval and military; by describing war as it exists at present, not in the costume of Ajax and Diomede."[52] The *Westminster Review* judged that Campbell needed to be forgiven for having written "Theodric," which seldom rises above "indifferent prose."[53] The *London Literary Gazette*, before "Theodric" was officially published, carried a report of the poem with extensive quotations but left readers to form their own opinions.[54] Its American counterpart, the *United States Literary Gazette*, considered that Campbell "has always been, and from the nature of things always must be, a popular poet, but, as it has been decided, a poet of the second class." Many passages in his works evoke "feelings inherent in human nature," but in "Theodric," which is "carelessly told," he failed where he "could have worked up this simple tale powerfully" and where the Lake poets would have succeeded. In coming now, however, "Theodric" will not shake Campbell's "well established reputation."[55]

Cyrus Redding noted of "Theodric" (which he misspelled "Theodoric"): "There is much of the author's character of mind in the poem. It commences with an energy and elegance which diminish as the poem proceeds, and soon become exhausted."[56] One reason for the inferiority of "Theodric," Redding felt, is that in it, perhaps unintentionally, Campbell "inclined much more in style to the modern taste in poetry than the 'Pleasures of Hope.' "[57]

Redding and Hadden both echoed Beattie in holding that some allowance should be made for Campbell's distractions about the mental illness of his son during the composition of "Theodric." Hadden also agreed with Redding that Campbell made a mistake in attempting to imitate Crabbe and Wordsworth.[58] Aytoun went further, saying that "with *Theodric* . . . [Campbell's] poetical career may be said to have closed."[59] After 1824, his health and outlook indeed permitted very little original poetry of any significance.

IV "The Pilgrim of Glencoe"

In his old age, Campbell turned to his homeland for the setting of his last long poem, a largely senile effort of his dying muse. As could be expected, his lifelong problems persist: poor punctuation, abruptness of narration, and obscure passages. The ingredients are those he had earlier known or used: Scottish history and landscape, interest in the military, heroic warriors, a family living in a remote dwelling visited by an outsider, democratic philosophy, exemplary womanhood, death, and sentiment. The story itself, based on tradition, is one Scott could have chosen.

Like Campbell's three other long poems, "The Pilgrim of Glencoe" begins with sunset over a wide landscape, this one described with a familiar love of the Western Highlands of Argyllshire. His success in portrayal is quite varied, from his beautiful description of the Scottish mists:

> But, looking at Ben Nevis, capped with snow,
> He saw its mists come curling down below
> And spread white darkness o'er the sunset glow—
> Fast rolling like tempestuous Ocean's spray,
> Or clouds from troops in battle's fiery day (ll. 53–57),

to his ludicrously alliterative seascape:

> While, gay with gambols of its finny shoals,
> The glancing wave rejoices as it rolls
> With streamered busses that distinctly shine
> All downward pictured in the glassy brine (ll. 3–6).

The intruder this time is an old veteran "of thirty fought campaigns" who "well could vouch the sad romance of wars" (ll. 20–21). Nine times wounded in battle, he enjoys telling his adventures, sketching such scenes as

> The wide war-plain, with banners glowing bright,
> And bayonets to the farthest stretch of sight;
> The pause, more dreadful than the peal to come
> From volleys blazing at the beat of drum,
> Till all the fields of thundering lines became
> Two level and confronted sheets of flame (ll. 41–46).

Stranded by a dense fog before he can reach his destination, the soldier-pilgrim gropes his way to a nearby cottage, a comfortable one such as Campbell himself lived in during his stay at Downie. There he is welcomed with highland hospitality, no questions asked about his name or itinerary.

A Jacobite white rose above the door reveals the political loyalty of the family—an old father, his son, and his daughter-in-law. Norman Macdonald is well drawn as a "proudly savage" old Jacobite, reminiscent of Scott's Baron Bradwardine in *Waverley*, a man who acts his emotions. His son Ronald, who grew up in "far happier times," rationally condemns "strife as childishness" and wonders whether "men were made for kings or kings for men" (l. 165). This line of reasoning has brought him to "flat . . . [deny] the Stuarts' right to sway" (l. 167), much to his father's rage. Inclined to study and learn from all available sources, Ronald enjoys hearing the visitor's stories; and "who pleased her Ronald ne'er displeased his wife" (l. 197).

The traveler turns out to be Allan Campbell, who in his youth had taken an unwilling part in the infamous massacre of the Macdonald clan at Glencoe, led by his Campbell chieftain and the English troops. For revengeful old Norman, the revelation that he is harboring beneath his roof a sworn enemy is too much to endure. He calls Ronald out to inform him that he intends to " 'sacrifice / The caitiff ere to-morrow's sun arise' " (ll. 276–77). At this climactic point, Ronald has to beseech his father not " 'to act at once the assassin and the fool' " (l. 287). A violation of hospitality would be a very serious offense; moreover, one punishable in modern days by " 'judge and jury, rope and gallows-tree' " (l. 301). But wrath will not listen, and Ronald succeeds only in temporizing: " 'Come in; till night put off the deed, / And ask a few more questions ere he bleed' " (ll. 312–13). In the tense, ironic conversation that ensues, Allan chances to reveal the satisfaction he has felt through the years from saving a mother and child he had been assigned to kill at Glencoe. Immediately Ronald realizes " 'That woman was my mother—I the child!' " (l. 347). In Campbell's rapid narration, "the old lion then / Upstarted, metamorphosed" (ll. 352–53), to offer Allan a home for his lifetime.

The next morning at sunrise, Allan, not quite ready to become a "fireside fixture," reveals that he is on his way to petition the Duke of Argyle for a pension. Ronald, understanding his desire and realizing that a Jacobite and a Hanoverian could not live together amicably at that time, assists Allan in wording his memorial to the duke and sends him on his way with a purse of gold coins, promising a like gift to be made annually. At Inverary, Argyle rewards Allan with a pension, a promotion to sergeant, and the news of the approach of Bonnie Prince Charlie's forces. Of course, Allan stays to help fight the invaders.

"Meanwhile the old choleric shepherd of Glencoe" (l. 458), spurning all pleadings to the contrary, plans to join the prince, until his high blood pressure "an artery in his wise sensorium burst" (l. 469). He lingers "in this lamentable state" (l. 476) long enough for Allan to return and describe for him (but not for the reader) the battle of Culloden. Norman laments, " 'It might not have been so had I been there!' " (l. 487). After the old Jacobite's ensuing death and burial on "the wild and lonely heath" (l. 489), Allan makes his home with Ronald and enjoys "a patriarchal age." At the end this Campbell is buried "with many a tear" (l. 501) near the house of his hosts, the Macdonalds.

In a note to the poem, Campbell admits that "perhaps relations of my great-grandfather . . . might be indirectly concerned in the cruelty" (p. 135). Even though "children," he holds, "are not answerable," this poem of reconciliation still partly expiates the crimes of his anti-Jacobite forefathers. In another way also, Campbell undoubtedly identified with the old men in the poem: he too, like Tennyson's Ulysses, was trying to prove that "old age hath yet his honour and his toil," and that "though much is taken, much abides."[60]

As might be expected, "The Pilgrim of Glencoe" did not excite the critics. In fact, most of them ignored it. *Blackwood's,* the *Edinburgh,* the *Quarterly,* the *Westminster,* and even the *New Monthly* said nothing about it. The *Athenaeum* summarized and quoted the "simple and interesting" story without judgment.[61] The *Spectator* stated: "Compared with the author's former productions, this volume is rather an amusement than a work; the occupation of a veteran, in a pursuit which long exercise has rendered easy, rather than the laborious struggles of a soldier in his prime, striving after victory." The reviewer considered "The Pilgrim" and its companion poems better mechanically than "some of his middle-aged productions: nor is the publication, in parts and passages, wanting in the higher qualities of art—in nature, truth, and beauty. The deficiency of the volume is in subject and matter." The story does not "constitute a *fable:* it has scarcely a beginning, still less a middle or an end," and it lacks "incident, purpose, or variety." Still, the "form" is good, with scenes and characters well sketched. "Old Norman, especially, is painted with thorough knowledge of the Highlander, and with what

Scott wanted, the philosophy to estimate him truly."[62]

The reviewer for the *Literary Gazette*, probably its editor, William Jerdan, regretted that despite his high esteem for the writer, he had to tell the truth: "By nothing of the kind were we ever so forcibly impressed with the image of the flickering of expiring flame, as we are by the bright momentary flashes, the smoky dulness, and the irregular fits of sinking, exhibited in these pages." Campbell's "childishness of mind" shows in his "slovenly style," "repetition and clicking of words and sounds," "queer beginning," "risible suggestions" in phrases and thoughts, repetitions of rhyme, and prosaic writing. "There are, however, some sparkles of Campbell."[63]

The *Monthly Review* judged the story "extremely simple, even to baldness, as respects incident as well as involution." In his criticisms, the writer echoed the faults cited in the *Spectator* and the *Literary Gazette* but concluded that in all, the poem "deserves to be bound up with the performances that established his reputation."[64]

The *Eclectic Review* made the point that Campbell's previous long poems had proved "that the Author's forte did not lie in the management of poetic narrative," and that he was "so exclusively as well as pre-eminently a lyrical poet, that he could succeed in no other kind."[65] In "Theodric," his failure had shown him "so unconscious of the secret of his strength as not to know when it had departed from him." "The Pilgrim of Glencoe," however, is "decidedly superior in interest, and in vigour of execution, to 'Theodric' " (p. 713). The reviewer judged the story "worthy of poetry, as being connected with traits of national manners which are fading away into tradition," and he found the characters "distinctly portrayed and skilfully discriminated." Ordinary readers, unfamiliar with the scene, however, might think the notes "more interesting than the text" (pp. 713–14).

The conclusion of the article is itself sentimental:

In closing these pages, we feel as if receiving a farewell from one whose visits, 'few and far between,' have yielded delight to every lover of poetry, and have secured to the Author a name that will not die so long as the English language survives. The contents of this publication will neither raise nor detract from his reputation. They are autumn blossoms, which do not aspire to rival in their hues the flowers of summer, but are welcomed for their lateness, and mourned because they are the last (p. 716).

He was right; they were.

CHAPTER 3

"Hearts of Oak": The Songs of Battle

I "Ye Mariners of England: a Naval Ode"

C AMPBELL'S lasting fame today rests primarily on his war songs,
especially "Ye Mariners of England," "Battle of the Baltic," and
"Hohenlinden," all three of which are products of his German period.
Few other poets have equaled him in writing blood-stirring poems of
nationalism and patriotism, epitomizing the spirit of his age and his
country. To Campbell, as to many Englishmen, the appeal of the sea
was strong; so was the belief in the importance of English sea power.
The first of his famous naval odes, "Ye Mariners of England," he
"composed on the prospect of a Russian War," according to part of its
original title in the *Morning Chronicle* in 1801. Begun in Edinburgh
in 1799, after a musical soirée, as new words to "Ye Gentlemen of
England," its spirited rhetoric can be sung as well as said.

The four stanzas of the poem constitute an extended apostrophe to
England's navy men to carry on the proud tradition of their fathers'
heroism. It is an oratorical lyric, appealing to manliness and exertion
of military might and projecting Campbell's underlying sense of his
own active nature and that of his responding readers. Each ten-line
stanza has only two hard-hitting masculine rhymes, with the second
of the two repeated: "seas," "breeze"; "foe," "blow," "blow." The
lines are short, alternating iambic tetrameter and trimeter; in each
stanza, the seventh line uses internal masculine rhyme with only two
galloping anapestic feet. Alliteration adds to the emphasis. The
assonance of the repeated *o* sounds and the repetition of the phonetic
intensive *blow* in all four stanzas suggest the sounds both of battle
and of the wind, with "the stormy winds" an effective metaphor for
war.[1]

To some readers, the poem may be only a piece of jingoistic flag-waving, but persons who like military poetry and respond to naval glory appreciate its spirit and enjoy the allusions to Robert Blake and Horatio Nelson, heroic British admirals who epitomized naval courage. In the first edition of the poem Sir Richard Grenville was the hero; after the Battle of Trafalgar in 1805, Nelson was substituted and Blake added. "Towers along the steep" alludes to the current fortification of the Straits of Dover with Martello towers. The poem's statement that these towers are not needed inspirits the courage of offense rather than resignation to defense. "The meteor flag of England" burning in "danger's troubled night" has been much admired as a metaphor referring both to the color of the flag and to the old superstition that meteors portend disaster, in this case for England's enemies. Yet the end of the poem anticipates the return of peace and its celebration with "song and feast."

"Christopher North," in *Blackwood's,* jokingly chided Campbell's lack of nautical expression. "Campbell has written the two finest sea-songs in the world. Yet 'Ye Mariners of England' might, we think, have been all that it is, and more an Ode of the Sea. The language is too much that of pure poetry. . . . A very few of the finest sea words would have glorified it exceedingly." To him, "The meteor flag of England," although "a grand image," is "not nautical." Pretending to be a literalist who relishes the discovery of blemishes in the poem, he laughs that Britain's home is not "on the deep" but on the land; moreover, harbors do need the protection of forts. Even so, "We would most willingly live a thousand years in purgatory to have written that song."[2]

Among the many admirers of the energy, enthusiasm, and sentiment of this ode were Thomas Carlyle and Washington Irving. Francis Jeffrey called it "a splendid instance of the most magnificent diction adapted to a familiar and even trivial metre," with "nothing . . . finer than the first and the last stanzas."[3] Walter Scott referred to "Ye Mariners of England" and "Battle of the Baltic" as "two beautiful war odes . . . [which] afford pleasing instances of that short and impetuous lyric sally in which Mr. Campbell excels all his contemporaries."[4]

II   *"Battle of the Baltic"*

Campbell's second great naval hymn deals with the Battle of Copenhagen of April 2, 1801, which he almost witnessed. The excitement of seeing the preparations from shipboard as he fled the hostilities is reflected in this ode celebrating Nelson's victory. After composing the poem in the winter of 1804–1805, Campbell wrote to Dr. James Currie on April 24, 1805, that the style of the thirty stanzas "is out of my beaten way. It is an attempt to write an English ballad on the battle of Copenhagen, as much as possible in that plain, strong style peculiar to our old ballads, which tells us the when, where, and how the event happened—without gaud or ornament but what the subject essentially and easily affords" (Beattie, 1:385). He did not copy the poem for Currie's inspection, but in a letter to Scott on March 27 that year, he copied a version "in its *incorrect* state" consisting of twenty-seven six-line stanzas. (This letter is still extant in the National Library of Scotland.) Beattie printed them as "The Battle of Copenhagen," as do Hill and Robertson in their editions of the collected works. Scott's reply, not extant, must have encouraged Campbell to shorten the piece. The resulting "Battle of the Baltic," in eight stanzas, first appeared in book form along with "Gertrude of Wyoming," but Jeffrey thought the poem had been printed before (probably in the newspapers).[5]

The nine lines of each stanza vary in length and rhythm. The prevailing trochaic tetrameter changes in the first line to iambic trimeter, in the fifth line to iambic pentameter with a metrical pause, and in the last line to dimeter—actually only three syllables, with the first and last ones stressed. The longer fifth line serves to slow the movement and to give perspective to the scene. The last short line not only stops each stanza completely but also adds a touch of ironic finality suggesting the temporariness of the pauses in battle. Critics who have wrongly objected to the short line include Jeffrey, who thought the meter "strange" and "unfortunate" but felt that the poem still "has great force and grandeur, both of conception and expression." It is "simple and concise," with events represented clearly and energetically so that the reader feels "all the terror and sublimity of the subject" without "the fatigue and perplexity of its details."[6]

The stanzas of the poem are logically arranged—the first shows the theme and the readiness of the Danes; the second presents the English anticipating the battle. The third has the beginning of the cannonading; the fourth, the defeat of the Danes; the fifth, the victors demanding their submission; the sixth, the return of peace; the seventh, the victory celebration in England; and the eighth, the condolence for the dead heroes, a reminder of the human cost of victory. The beginning of the poem prays a muse, or someone, to "sing the glorious day's renown" (st. 1) and the end has the mermaid's song "singing glory to the souls / Of the brave!" (st. 8).

Like Dr. Beattie, Cyrus Redding thought "Battle of the Baltic" the best of Campbell's odes, calling it "a piece of action, addressed to more senses than one," with the sound "truly an echo to the sense." The repetition of "again" at the beginning of the fourth stanza makes the sound of the heavy firing seem "like the real thing." To him, "Every stanza is a natural and perfect painting of itself, so that an artist might sketch from it a distinct feature. . . . In fact, the whole is unequalled in our language."[7]

The rhyme scheme of each stanza contributes to the overall effect. The first four lines alternate, with a new rhyme in the long fifth line that is not repeated until the short last line. The sixth, seventh, and eighth lines share the d rhyme, which serves to build suspense for the final crash of the remembered c rhyme of line five. Thus, the long line is paired with the short line not only by rhyme but, in several stanzas, by sense; an example is in stanza eight: "Soft sigh the winds of Heaven o'er their grave! . . . Of the brave!"

The success of the poem is due largely to its concentration of martial energy and enthusiasm. Changing it from a ballad to an oratorical lyric eliminated monotony, chauvinism, repetition, and unnecessary detail and increased its dignity. The earlier and later versions are a study in the art of poetry.

Set to music, the ode was very popularly sung. One musical version by Gerard Manley Hopkins has two choirs singing in unison—the first choir, the British; the second, the Danes. Two songs are in the background of the poem. The battle cry " 'Hearts of oak!' " in the third stanza Campbell took from the old song "Ye Gentlemen of England." At the time he wrote the piece, he may have had in mind also a popular Danish song about King Christian and Niels Juel valiantly defeating the Swedes, according to a *Quarterly* reviewer.[8]

The music-conscious Tennyson liked Campbell's odes, but he considered "the mermaid's song condoles" of the last stanza of "Battle of the Baltic" to be "infelicitous."[9] Some influence of Campbell's poem is observable in Tennyson's "Ballad of the Fleet" and in Browning's "Hervé Riel." As a boy, Carlyle was much impressed by it and by "Hohenlinden." Washington Irving considered "Ye Mariners of England" and "Battle of the Baltic" "two of the noblest national songs we have ever seen . . . , but totally free from that hyperbole and national rhodomontade which generally disgrace this species of poetry." With "Hohenlinden" and "Lochiel's Warning" they are sufficient, Irving thought, "to establish his [Campbell's] title to the sacred name of Poet."[10]

Even J. Cuthbert Hadden calls the poem "one of the finest and most enduring war-songs in the language" and "one of the few vigorous battle pieces we have." He judges its meter "really one of its merits," with the unequal lengths of line relieving monotony and "the sharp, short final line . . . an excellent invention." Invariably, however, Hadden's compliments must be accompanied by a barb: "The poem has defects in plenty . . . : not a stanza would pass muster to-day."[11]

One reason Hopkins was attracted to "Battle of the Baltic" was that in it he found a simple form of sprung rhythm, an oratorical rhythm that he defined as "*abrupt*" and applying "only where one stress follows another running, without syllable between."[12] An example is "Ańd their fléet alońg the *deép proúdly* shóne."[13] Hopkins liked Campbell's handling of rhythm and regretted that he did not continue to experiment with a new music for English poetry. Still, he held Campbell "a perfect master of style,"[14] concurring with Matthew Arnold's opinion in his essay "On the Study of Celtic Literature." To Hopkins,

Cold and dull as the *Pleasures of Hope* is and much more that he wrote, there is always the "freehand" of a master in his work beyond almost all our poets, and when one turns from his frigidities to what are held his masterpieces and will always keep his name green, the *Battle of the Baltic* and so forth, one finds a kind of spirited felicity seen no where else that he himself could not have analyzed or justified. An inversion and a phrase like 'On the deck of fame that died' or the lines 'But the might of England flushed To anticipate the scene' seem to me as if the words had fallen into their places at a magic signal and not by any strain and continuance of thought.[15]

III   *"Hohenlinden"*

Campbell's third popular martial lyric is a generalized picture of the land battle at the Bavarian village of Hohenlinden, east of Munich, where the French defeated the Austrians on December 3, 1800. Its eight concise tetrameter quatrains catch the sounds of warfare and the human response to it without involving any political feelings. The authenticity of the poem is due to Campbell's own haunting view of the horrors of the capture of Ratisbon, his sight of the ruins of Ingolstadt soon after the battle there, and recollections of his visit to Hohenlinden about six weeks before the battle. Perhaps he chose Hohenlinden as the most poetic name, especially when shortened to Linden to fit his iambic meter. He could also use the two-syllable river Iser (Isar) as part of the landscape and as a symbol.

The statement of the poem is direct and positive; its vigorous and energetic movement captures the excitement of battle and its human cost—attraction and repulsion. It is both oratorical and lyrical. Heightening contrasts are the untouched natural scenery versus the martial activities of man and the light versus dark color imagery, making much use of red. The effective first stanza gives an ominous tone to the landscape, enhanced by the regular monotony of the meter and the assonance of the *o*s. The sun is "low," the "untrodden snow" is "bloodless," and the river, "rolling rapidly," is "dark as winter." Sunset and winter both suggest death, and the river, human life.

The second stanza replaces the light of sunset on the untrodden snow of Linden with the "fires of death to light / The darkness of her scenery" (ll. 7–8). Sound imagery comes in with the ominous "drum beat." Light and onomatopoetic sound combine in the third stanza with "torch" and "battle-blade," trumpets, furious neighing of chargers, and "dreadful revelry"—an appropriate cacophony. In the next stanza, the tempo increases as the hills shake with thunder, the steed rushes to battle, and the "red artillery" flashes "louder than the bolts of heaven" (l. 15). By the fifth stanza, the light is glowing red, the untrodden snow has become the "stained snow," and the river, still "rolling rapidly," is "bloodier yet." When morning comes, the "level sun" can scarcely "pierce the war-clouds, rolling dun" (l. 22), creating a "sulph'rous canopy." Man thus pollutes nature with his war.

In the last three stanzas, the "furious Frank, and fiery Hun" (l. 23) shout, wave their banners, and "charge" with their "chivalry." (Note that these two words are pronounced alliteratively with the hard *ch* sound.) "On, ye brave, / Who rush to glory, or the grave!" (ll. 25–26). But what is the price of all this heroism? Futility: "Few, few, shall part where many meet!" (l. 29) In the quiescent ending, the eternally present snow becomes "their winding sheet, / And every turf beneath their feet / Shall be a soldier's sepulchre" (ll. 30–32). Like the other battle pieces, "Hohenlinden" ends with a tone of sympathy for the fallen. This ambivalence, the glory of heroic achievement sobered by the loss of those very heroes, constitutes the affective tension of the powerful poem.

The rhyme scheme contributes to the rapidity of movement and to the sound effects. The first three lines of each stanza repeat the same rhyme, always masculine except at the peak of battle in the fourth stanza, where the feminine rhymes "riven," "driven," and "heaven" increase the rapidity of action. The "glow"—"snow"—"flow" and "sun"—"dun"—"Hun" of the fifth and sixth stanzas imitate the sounds of cannons. The last lines of all stanzas rhyme with one another in feminine half-rhyme: "rapidly," "scenery," "canopy," and so forth. (The final "sepulchre" approximates the others, yet differs enough to spring a touch of irony.) These half-rhymes function as a lighter contrast to the heavy thrust of the first three lines, carry the motion forward, and with their final long *e* sound, echo the scream of artillery shells. The two kinds of rhyme, repeated in this regular pattern, add another contrast to the ironic dichotomy of meaning: masculine aggressiveness and feminine tenderness.

Campbell composed "Hohenlinden" in 1802 and printed it anonymously with "Lochiel," both dedicated to the Reverend Archibald Alison. The poet later reprinted them in the "Gertrude" volume in 1809, where they attracted favorable notice. Scott in the *Quarterly* mentioned them as "splendid poems . . . manifesting high powers of imagination."[16] The *Eclectic Review* pronounced them "perhaps the master pieces of Mr. Campbell's muse; each is *unique*, and may be for ever unrivalled."[17] The *London Review* likewise termed "Hohenlinden" "probably superior to every thing of its kind."[18] Jeffrey called it "the only representation of a modern battle, which possesses either interest or sublimity."[19] To the *British Critic*, "the concluding stanza in particular . . . offers an uncommon specimen of the power of giving a great result in very few words, and compressing almost an infinity of ideas into four lines."[20] Hazlitt praised it as "of all modern compositions the most lyrical in spirit and in sound."[21]

Washington Irving recorded a conversation he held with Scott during his visit to Abbotsford, in which Scott took part of the credit for Campbell's publishing "Hohenlinden": "And there's that glorious little poem, too, of Hohenlinden; after he had written it, he did not seem to think much of it, but considered some of it 'd—d drum and trumpet lines.' I got him to recite it to me, and I believe that the delight I felt and expressed had an effect in inducing him to print it."[22] If Scott's assumption is correct, as it probably is, the publication of a classic in English literature is the consequence of a friendship.

IV *Other Songs of Battle*

Campbell's other military poems, less successful, can be called either sentimental or sword-rattling. The better sentimental ones are "The Soldier's Dream" and "The Launch of a First-rate." The former was inspired by the sight of a Bavarian battlefield between Ratisbon and Ingolstadt in 1800. Again the theme is the harvest of war in human terms, and again the natural universe contrasts with the deeds of man. A poignant dream of home at harvest time opposes the reality of battle's harvest. Beginning as in other poems with the wide-angle view, where "the night-cloud had lowered, / And the sentinel stars set their watch in the sky" (ll. 1–2), the focus narrows to a closeup of a single soldier reposing on his "pallet of straw" and dreaming "a sweet vision." The nearby light in the darkened picture is a realistic "wolf-scaring faggot that guarded the slain" (l. 6). Another excellent touch of realism has often been quoted: "and thousands had sunk on the ground overpowered, / The weary to sleep, and the wounded to die" (ll. 3–4). In his dream the soldier pledges "never to part" again from home and loved ones, "but sorrow returned with the dawning of morn, / And the voice in my dreaming ear melted away" (ll. 23–24). It was 1804 before Campbell finished the poem and published it—an example of "emotion recollected in tranquillity."[23]

In his old age, Campbell's love for the navy inspired him to try another naval ode to express the excitement he felt when, as an invited guest, he witnessed the launch of two ships of war at Chatham on September 29, 1840. For his honor, the ceremony included the enthusiastic singing of "Ye Mariners of England" by a seventy-voice chorus. After the launch, the naval architect gave a dinner at which Campbell's health was toasted and a band played "The Campbells Are Coming!" Campbell said in his response: "Whatever my verses may be, their being sung at this spectacle connects me more nearly with my nation. I have always loved my mother country; but now I feel as if, by special endearment, she were pressing me closely to her maternal breast!' " (Beattie, 2:404). Later he wrote "The Launch of a First-Rate" about the second of the two vessels, the "London," a ship of the line mounting ninety-two guns. In his welcome to the "Mightiest child of naval art!" (l. 2) he speaks of the "seven hundred acres" of giant oaks felled to build its "noble mansion / Where our hearts of oak shall dwell" (ll. 7–8) (Here he reuses his "Hearts of oak!" from "Battle of the Baltic" and "thunders from her native oak" in "Ye Mariners of England.") The "native spirit" of those robust oaks, he imagines, will live on in the timbers of the ship, whose foes will flee as soon as they see it approaching.[24]

Beattie thought the lyric might "take its place with the best of his naval odes," (2:404), and in so stating, he was echoing the opinion of several critics who felt as kindly toward the poem as did the writer for the *Monthly Review*, who rejoiced that "Campbell's spirit is not quenched, nor his mastery lost."[25] Redding's comment is more realistic, though: "How quails the 'Launch of the first rate,' before his superb naval odes!"[26]

One of Campbell's most popular, and most sentimental, military lyrics became a street ballad that he was later ashamed to acknowledge. "The Wounded Hussar," written in 1797 when he was only twenty, before he went to Germany, is set on a battlefield along the Danube where "Fair Adelaide hied" seeking her lover Henry. Soon hearing his sigh, "on the heath she descried / By the light of the moon her poor wounded Hussar!" (ll. 7–8). Despite her tears and reassurances, nonetheless, he "sunk in her arms." In 1799, Campbell published it with the first edition of "The Pleasures of Hope." In 1802, the sophisticated young poet wrote to his oldest sister on November 13: " 'Pray send me word what *tune* is set to that accursed song, 'The Wounded Hussar,' which freezes my blood with the recollection of its being sung in Queen Street. Wretch that I am; *that* circumstance is still a joke among my friends! I believe it will disturb my dying moments—for it is never to be forgotten!' " (1:332). Beattie comments that "in after years, . . . this morbid sensitivity wore off" (1:332).

As a contemporary of Napoleon Bonaparte and as an English champion of freedom, Campbell had much to say about the " 'angry little savage,' " as he termed him in a letter to Alison (Beattie, 1:346). At the time of public excitement over the fear of a French invasion in 1803, when Campbell himself had enlisted in the North British Volunteers, he felt called upon to play the role of Tyrtaeus and address his "fellow freemen" with "Stanzas on the Threatened Invasion, 1803." "To arms! oh my Country, to arms!" he cried (l. 16). All four stanzas conclude with the same refrain: "Then rise, fellow freemen, and stretch the right hand, / And swear to prevail in your dear native land!"

Waterloo inspired two songs: "Troubadour Song on the Morning of the Battle of Waterloo" (written for June 18, 1815) and "Song" (written about 1822). The troubadour addresses his "saint" or his "mistress" (he calls her both) to assure her that she will never need blush for his honor; he goes "content to the combat" knowing that his name will live "in the shrine of . . . [her] breast!" (l. 24). The "Song," beginning "When Napoleon was flying / From the field of Waterloo," is the sentimental farewell of a dying British soldier to his brother and through him to the maiden he loves.

Late in his life, about 1840, Campbell told one of the apocryphal stories about Napoleon, supposedly true: "Napoleon and the British Sailor." It begins:

> I love contemplating, apart
>   From all his homicidal glory,
> The traits that soften to our heart
>   Napoleon's story.

The protagonist of the humorous action is a captured British sailor who manages to construct a wretched vessel of barrel staves and wattled willows in which he boldly intends to cross the English Channel. Captured in the act of launching it and taken before Napoleon, he explains so simply that he was longing to see his mother that Napoleon rewards him with a gold piece, a flag of truce, and passage to England. The poetry is worse than the sentiment.

Freedom for the Greeks and for the Spaniards received two sword-waving songs each, in addition to those for the Poles and the Germans. "Song of the Greeks," written for the *New Monthly Magazine* in 1822, shows that Campbell shared Byron's interest in their cause. It begins:

> Again to the battle, Achaians!
> Our hearts bid the tyrants defiance;
> Our land, the first garden of Liberty's tree—
> It has been, and shall yet be, the land of the free!

Campbell's imaginary speaker rallies his countrymen to fight the Turks, even though such Christian countries as England refuse to help. "We'll perish or conquer more proudly alone" (l. 14), fighting "as heroes descended from heroes" (l. 40). His extreme desires are that "the footprints of Mahomet's slaves / May be washed out in blood from our forefathers' graves!" (ll. 7–8), and that "the blood of yon Mussulman cravens / Shall have purpled the beaks of our ravens" (ll. 49–50).

After the Battle of Navarino, October 20, 1827, when Sir Edward Codrington led the allied British, French, and Russian fleets to annihilate the Turkish and Egyptian navies, Campbell celebrated the national feeling in "Stanzas on the Battle of Navarino" (1828), rejoicing that the "Hearts of oak" had "uplifted old Greece from the brink of the grave" (ll. 1–2). In the poem he silenced all critics and concluded with "Glory to Codrington's name!" In a comment on these seven stanzas, which he called "a rumble-tumble concern," Campbell considered his ability to write anything at all a symptom of his recovery from a liver ailment. " 'My *ingine,* as the Scotch call their genius, is not certainly reinspired to any very high pitch—to judge by my Navarino stuff' " (Beattie, 2:201).

Campbell published both Spanish poems in the *New Monthly* in 1823. The first, "The Spanish Patriot's Song," has the anti-Bourbon singer urging his fellows to "Shake the Spanish blade, and sing— / France shall ne'er enslave us: / Tyrants shall not brave us" (ll. 38–40). He also refers to "yonder rag, the Bourbon's flag," as the "white emblem of his liver" (ll. 17–18). For writing that line, "Timothy Tickler" of *Blackwood's* rebuked Campbell, holding it "not fit for a gentleman like Campbell to fall into the filthy slang of the blackguards of the press."[27]

"Stanzas to the Memory of the Spanish Patriots Latest Killed in Resisting the Regency and the Duke of Angoulême" cheered the resisters to the French invaders trying to free Ferdinand VII of Spain from the Spanish liberals. As did many Englishmen, Campbell encouraged the supporters of the constitution: "Hope is not withered in affliction's blast— / The patriot's blood's the seed of Freedom's tree" (ll. 12–13). Despite the momentary victory of the "cowled Demons of the Inquisitorial cell" (l. 15), "vengeance is behind, and justice is to come" (l. 45). Moreover, "There is a victory in dying well / For Freedom" (ll. 3–4).

In his review of the "Theodric" volume, which included "Stanzas to the Memory of the Spanish Patriots," Francis Jeffrey rejoiced that Campbell in "hatred of oppression" had "held on his course." "It is a proud thing indeed for England, for poetry, and for mankind, that all the illustrious poets of the present day—Byron, Moore, Rogers, Campbell—are distinguished by their zeal for freedom, and their scorn for courtly adulation."[28]

In "Ode to the Germans" (1832) Campbell spoke for his country:

> The Spirit of Britannia
>   Invokes across the main
> Her sister Allemannia
>   To burst the tyrant's chain (ll. 1–4).

He contrasts the two countries in that

> With Freedom's lion-banner
> Britannia rules the waves;
> Whilst your broad stone of honour
> Is still the camp of slaves (ll. 11–14).

The Germans should wake "for shame, for glory's sake" (l. 15).

"Lines on Poland" (1831) requires one hundred fifty-seven lines of heroic verse to express Campbell's indignation about the struggle of his Polish friends and the failure of England, France, and Germany to "chide . . . the Imperial Thief," Russia. Certainly England could send the fleet "to warm the insulter's seas with barbarous blood / And interdict his flag from ocean's flood" (ll. 119–20). He concludes that "younger bards, and nobler lyres" should resume the praise of Poland expiring from his "faltering lips." Not yet having had his say on the subject, however, later that same year he printed "The Power of Russia," eleven Spenserian stanzas of polemic, in the *Metropolitan*. Although he called it " 'a strange subject for verse,' " he explained that he had begun " 'to think that men reason better in verse than in prose—in rhyme than in reason' " (Beattie, 2:261). What he wrote was only rhymed prose, not poetry.

In the same vein, he addressed more verses "To Sir Francis Burdett on his speech delivered in Parliament, August 7, 1832, respecting the foreign policy of Great Britain." In them he commended Burdett for chiding "our slumbering statesmen" for their softness against Russian despotism.

Not often did Campbell agree to write a poem upon request, but one he did reluctantly produce waves both sword and thistle: "Lines Written at the Request of the Highland Society in London, When Met to Commemorate the 21st of March, the Day of Victory in Egypt, 1809." Campbell called it " 'verses on the glory of the "kilted clans," and on the military fame of poor old Scotland' " (Beattie, 1:517)—specifically the heroism of Sir John Moore and of the 42nd Highland Regiment (the Black Watch). Such men are "Types of a race who shall to time unborn / Their country leave unconquer'd as of yore!" (ll. 39–40). "Triumphant be the thistle still unfurl'd, / Dear symbol wild!" (ll. 21–22) is one toast to his homeland, "Invincible romantic Scotia's shore!" (l. 2). "Peace to the mighty dead" (l. 17) shows his concern for the price of heroism.

"Song: 'Men of England,' " first published in the *New Monthly*

Magazine in 1822, has been popular. Another patriotic military poem evoking the archetypal character of the hero, it shifts its point of view. The first six stanzas are a didactic address to the "Men of England"; for instance,

> Yet, remember, England gathers
>   Hence but fruitless wreaths of fame,
> If the freedom of your fathers
>   Glow not in your hearts the same (ll. 9–12).

Then the last stanza is written in first person identification:

> We're the sons of sires that baffled
>   Crowned and mitred tyranny:—
> They defied the field and scaffold
>   For their birthrights—so will we!

Campbell's strangest song of battle is "The Death-Boat of Heligoland," written in 1828, the year of his wife's death and his son's continued mental illness. Based on a Scandinavian legend, it too has an archetypal theme, a search for peace beyond life. Like Coleridge's "ghastly crew" in "The Rime of the Ancient Mariner," this story has a boat sailed by a crew of dead sleepwalkers, those "that dream in the tomb / And that maddening forehear the last trumpet of doom, / Till their corses start sheeted to revel on earth" (ll. 3–5), or "at mid-sea appal the chilled mariner's glance" (l. 8). This "band of cadaverous smile" was "seen ploughing the night-surge of Heligo's isle" (ll. 9–10) in the North Sea, "high bounding from billow to billow" (l. 17)—with the help of an anapestic tetrameter rhythm. The picture of the spectre-ship is set off by the foam sparkling like fire, by the red moon whose beams "on a sudden grew sick-like and gray" (l. 12), and by "the buoys and the beacons extinguish[ing] their light" (l. 15) at its approach. Sound effects are the clanging and shrieking of mews, the blood-curdling shouts of the "stony-eyed dead" to "the challenging watchman," and then the clang of "the old abbey bell." The guilt-haunted wanderers, each with "its shroud like a plaid flying loose to the storm" (l. 18), announce that they " 'are bound from . . . [their] graves in the west, / First to Hecla, and then to _____,' " but "unmeet was the rest / For man's ear" (ll. 25–27). Before they vanish, they stop long enough to be recognized, but the poet identifies them only as a "faction" whose badge was not green,

   . . . men who had trampled and tortured and driven
To rebellion the fairest isle breathed on by Heaven,—
Men whose heirs would yet finish the tyrannous task,
If the Truth and the Time had not dragged off their mask (ll. 37–40).

At the end the poet declines to blot his page with their name. They could be the Irish Orangemen, but the subconscious spell of the macabre poem is more effective without identification of the mysterious strangers.

CHAPTER 4

The Cast of Shadows: Poems Historical and Legendary

THE poems that the Oxford edition of Campbell's *Poetical Works* classifies as "Historical and Legendary" are largely Scottish. Less successful on the whole than the war songs, they are nonetheless memorable in theme.

The best-known one is "Lochiel's Warning" (1801), a dialogue in anapestic couplets between a wizard who has the gift of "second sight" and Lochiel, a Scottish highland chieftain whose actual name is Donald Cameron. The time is shortly before the Jacobite uprising of 1745, and Lochiel, remembered as "the gentle Lochiel" for his "social virtues," is now showing the other side of his character, "his martial and magnanimous (though mistaken) loyalty," as Campbell phrases it in his notes following poem (p. 161). He has dedicated himself to the Stuart cause, which is soon to be lost at the field of Culloden, and his influence will determine the decisions of the other highland chiefs..

In their exchange, the wizard, similar to Gray's "Bard," tries to warn Lochiel of his coming defeat:

> Lochiel, Lochiel! beware of the day;
> For, dark and despairing, my sight I may seal,
> But man cannot cover what God would reveal.
> 'Tis the sunset of life gives me mystical lore,
> And coming events cast their shadows before (ll. 52–56).[1]

The wizard sees the "field of the dead," the fleeing clansmen, and the wounded and slain trampled by Cumberland's horsemen. He also predicts the wounding of Lochiel and the bloodhound-pursued flight of Prince Charles, concluding with a vivid description of death by hanging for prisoners.

Lochiel's is the last word, however. His sense of honor and scorn of cowardice have overcome his wisdom and driven him to a search for glory. Having been won over to the hopeless cause by the personal appeal of the prince, he calls the wizard "false," tells him "I trust not the tale" (l. 78), and goes off to win or to die, "leaving in battle no blot on his name" (l. 87). He will "look proudly to Heaven from the death-bed of fame" (l. 88).

Campbell, still basking in the warmth of the success of "The Pleasures of Hope" and anxious to live up to his reputation, circulated the poem in manuscript among several of his friends, including Dr. Currie, Dugald Stewart, Allison, Lord Minto, and Scott, and solicited their opinions. All gave them. Minto as well as others thought the description of hanging vulgar, but Campbell defended the passage as " 'heightening the horror of the wizard's address' " (Beattie, 1:320). His agitation in trying to please everyone caused him to write several versions of the poem, some still extant. He did succeed in enlarging and improving it, however, and most of the critics have liked it.

Another poem dealing with a vision of death is the "Dirge of Wallace," which Campbell wrote in 1795 when he was only eighteen. Although definitely juvenile, it shows his early interest in the freedom-loving patriot. Sir William Wallace was a Scottish national hero executed by the English in 1305 for his resistance to the English king Edward I during the struggle for Scottish independence. Amidst Gothic omens that are "the warning of God," Wallace's wife, the "lady of Elderslie" has a nightmare that her husband "is doomed to die." The last four stanzas praise "the Wallace wight" for his military achievements and his glorious death for his country. Campbell, terming the poem "too rhapsodical," never revised it later or permitted it to appear in the London editions of his poetry, although it came out in the Paris editions. Redding felt Campbell's antipathy to it was "unaccountable."[2]

One of Campbell's best ballads, "Lord Ullin's Daughter," is based on a highland legend and set at the dangerous crossing from Mull to Ulva, which Campbell knew. He began the poem on Mull in 1795, completed it at Sydenham in 1804, and included it with "Gertrude of Wyoming" in 1809. Written in ballad stanza with alternate masculine and feminine rhymes, the traditional story has the lady and her lover, "the chief of Ulva's isle," fleeing the wrath of her pursuing father and his men. Although they succeed in persuading the boatman to row them across Lochgyle in the face of a storm, " 'Twas vain"; the stormy water proves "too strong from human hand." One good stanza describes the storm:

> By this the storm grew loud apace,
>> The water-wraith was shrieking;
> And in the scowl of heaven each face
>> Grew dark as they were speaking (ll. 25–28).

The old ballad "Sir Patrick Spens" is similar. Two of Scott's poems, "Lochinvar" and "Jock of Hazeldean," also tell stories of elopement, but his have happy endings. Campbell's is a memorable little tragedy that has been set to music and sung in many drawing rooms.

"Glenara" tells another traditional story that Campbell heard while he lived at Downie, Argyllshire, in 1797. Its anapestic tetrameter quatrains give the account of "fair Ellen of Lorn," married to the wrong man, Maclean of Duart (Glenara). He exposes her on the Lady Rock between Oban and Mull to drown with the rising tide, then pretends bereavement, and accordingly conducts a false funeral to which he has invited her kinsmen. Campbell's version has the lady's former true love dream the truth and demand that Glenara interpret his dream. When the coffin is revealed to be empty, justice is done instantly. Glenara is buried in Ellen's readymade grave, and the fair lady is rescued. Joanna Baillie's tragedy "The Family Legend" (1810) tells the same story. When Campbell published "Glenara" with "Gertrude" in 1809, Scott perceived "Glenara" an approach to "the rude yet forcible simplicity of the ancient minstrels," with Lord Ullin's Daughter" having "a more refined plan."[3] Jeffrey thought the two pieces both contained "very considerable merit," and presented "a favourable specimen of Mr Campbell's powers in this new line of exertion." "Lord Ullin's Daughter" he judged "the most beautiful."[4]

Gaelic lore from the island of Iona is the inspiration for "Reullura," which in Gaelic means "beautiful star." When he printed the poem in the *New Monthly* in 1824, Campbell attached a prefatory note explaining that the Culdees, Irish in origin, were "the primitive clergy of Scotland," and their monastery on Iona "was the seminary of Christianity in North Britain."[5] Unlike other religious orders at the time, they permitted their clergy to marry, and Reullura, the heroine of the piece, is the wife of the Culdee Aodh. The story is a saint's legend, the source of which is unknown; Campbell, however, was interested in the early Gaels and retained vivid memories of his visit to Iona from Mull in 1795.

Reullura is another of Campbell's characters with the gift of second sight who "oft saw / The veil of fate uplifted" (ll. 24–25). One evening, standing alone with Aodh "by the statue of an aged Saint," (l. 30), she tells Aodh that the saint will come to avenge her martyrdom and save Aodh and the remnant of the Gaels from the sword of the Danish raider Ulvfagre, whose ships are now approaching. In answer to Aodh's doubts, she explains that the saint lives, " 'For the span of his life tenfold extends / Beyond the wonted years of men' " (ll. 61–62). The prophecy comes true; that night the Danes arrive to murder and ravage. Aodh is captured; Reullura plunges dramatically into the sea "in pride" to mock "the men of blood"; the saint, "an agèd man of majestic height" (l. 128) enters, frees Aodh, stops the weapons of the Danes, and causes his statue to crush Ulvfagre. At dawn he gathers the "doleful remnant of the Gael" (l. 183) into his own ship while the Norse look on silently, and they depart for Innisfail (Ireland) without Reullura, whose "spirit was in heaven" (l. 195).

"Reullura" is not one of Campbell's better efforts. Many passages sound more like prose than poetry, with irregular rhythm, variable line lengths, and approximate rhymes like "similitude"—"stood" and "form"—"arm." One of the worst irregular passages is

> Nor word was spoken by one beholder,
> Whilst he flung his white robe back on his shoulder,
> And, stretching his arm, as eath
> Unriveted Aodh's bands
> As if the gyves had been a wreath
> Of willows in his hands (ll. 134–39).

Even sprung rhythm, if that was the poet's intention, should include the correct number of accents in the line. Also, some details of the story itself are unclear; for instance, why could some of the women and children escape into hiding while Reullura must plunge into the sea, a martyr?

The critics could say little good about the poem. The *Westminster Review* termed it "principally remarkable for combining all the metres in the English language (and a few more)."[6] Cyrus Redding held that "the importance which the poet endeavours to confer on the 'mailed swarms' of the North, fails of effect. There is not enough to arouse our sympathy, and unless that be excited, verse falls flat. The priests of Scotland in the sixth century are too remote for modern confraternity."[7]

"Gilderoy," published with "The Pleasures of Hope" in 1799, is a sentimental ballad depicting the grief of a widow for her hanged husband. At the time of his fatal hour, her thoughts return to the beginning of their love "in Roslin's lovely glen"; then she contemplates the future for a forlorn widow and her orphan boy, concluding that all she can do is weep at her husband's grave. The poem treats several themes Campbell used later: the separation of lovers, human suffering, and the endurance of woman. Although he wrote it hastily, he was willing to print it with his name attached.

Campbell's worst ballad is "The Ritter Bann," which he published in the *New Monthly* in 1824. Its mixture of nationalities resembles its hodgepodge of rhymes, metrics, sentiments, artificialities, and obscurities of narration. Even worse, it runs for one hundred seventy-six lines. A ritter is an Austrian or German knight, but Howel Bann is from Glamorganshire in Wales. His English cousin-wife Jane has a Scottish nurse whose son, serving on a ship in England, plays a part. The "Abbot of St. James's monks," who effects the reconciliation, is patterned after Dr. Arbuthnot, president of the Scotch College, a Benedictine monastery at Ratisbon, whose kindnesses to him there Campbell never forgot. The story takes place in a hotel room in Vienna after the "gloomy Ritter Bann" has just returned from Hungary "renowned in arms." The abbot brings in the old nurse, who, in the bathetic ending, recounts the wrongs done to both the knight and Jane; produces their son, whom the knight has never seen; and then reveals to him the still lovely Jane. Elements of the story of lovers reunited resemble many stories in literature, including Shakespeare's *Romeo and Juliet* and *The Winter's Tale* (Leontes and Hermione).

As might be expected, the poem became a target for Campbell's sharp young critical opponents in *Blackwood's,* who published "A Running Commentary on the Ritter Bann, a Poem, by T. Campbell, Esq." Pretending to be generous in noticing works in rival magazines, they quote most of the poem, write out parts of it as prose to show its lack of poetry, and intersperse comments all along. The first concerns the meaning of the title: "Why a Welsh knight should be called by a German title, we cannot immediately conjecture; but suppose it adopted from euphonious principles of melting melody." At the end of their presentation, they inquire: "Did anybody ever see the like? What verse, what ideas, what language, what a story, what a name! Time was, that, when the brains were out, the man would die; but *on a changé tout cela.* We consign Campbell's head to the notice of the Phrenologicals."[8]

The pathetic "O'Connor's Child; or, 'The Flower of Love-Lies-Bleeding' " is an Irish story that Campbell wrote at the end of 1809 and published early in 1810 with another edition of "Gertrude." "Considered," says Beattie, "by good judges, as the most highly finished of all his minor pieces," (1:525), it has also been judged "superior in pathos and passion, to his more elaborate compositions."[9] Washington Irving called it an "uncommonly spirited and affecting little tale."[10]

A flower in his own garden called love-lies-bleeding is supposed to have suggested the theme. "O'Connor's Child" is a historical narrative poem in the tradition of Scott's "Cadyow Castle" (1803), which Campbell liked very much, and of "The Lady of the Lake," which Scott was writing in 1809. Its tetrameter couplets tell the story of the daughter of the Irish house of O'Connor whose marriage to Connocht Moran does not conform to the pride of ancestry of her brothers. They pursue the happy couple to their rustic hideaway, murder their new brother-in-law, and receive the curse of their sister, who turns into a prophetess of doom, predicting the English conquest of Ireland. All of this is told by a harper to explain why the lady is now a madwoman living in the wilds beside her husband's grave, cherishing the first flower to grow thereon (a love-lies-bleeding), and fancying she communes with the dead.

"The Spectre Boat," subtitled "A Ballad," resembles the later "Death-Boat of Heligoland" with its theme of a ghostly sailor, but here the boat is "row'd by a woman in her shroud" (l. 11). The poem has psychological overtones of guilt and revenge, for "False Ferdinand" loved and left "a lovely maid forlorn," causing her to die "to hide her blushing cheek from scorn" (l. 2).

> One night he dreamt he woo'd her in their wonted bower
>   of love, . . .
> But the scene was swiftly changed into a church-yard's
>   dismal view,
> And her lips grew black beneath his kiss, from love's
>   delicious hue.
> What more he dreamt, he told to none; but shuddering,
>   pale, and dumb,
> Look'd out upon the waves, like one that knew his hour
>   was come (ll. 3–8).

In "the dead watch of the night," the boat appears in the Mediterranean in the glare of Mount Etna, which suggests the fires of hell. Its mistress calls: "Come, Traitor, down, for whom my ghost still wanders unforgiven!" (l. 13). Ferdinand cannot help himself; he plunges "to meet her call." The mariners

. . . shrunk daunted from the sight,
For the Spectre and her winding-sheet shone blue with hideous light;
Like a fiery wheel the boat spun with the waving of her hand,
And round they went, and down they went, as the cock crew from the land (ll. 17–20).

This last line has the effect of an incantation, with the crowing of the cock breaking the magic spell and banishing spectres to the underworld.

This ballad in dipodic verse also has resemblances to Coleridge's "Rime of the Ancient Mariner," but the myth is incomplete, ending in punishment without restoration. Only the crowing of the cock promises a new day. In his edition of the poem, W. A. Hill affixes a note saying: "It requires no small effort of genius to amalgamate in any degree the natural with the unnatural; to reconcile the simplicity of the pastoral ballad with the strange medleys and unreality of an indistinct vision of the night! How artistically Campbell could arrange his *reconciliations*, and keep within the conceded tether of poetic license, is apparent from the preceding stanzas."[11]

Interestingly, the poem originated in a dream, as Campbell explained in a letter: " 'I am trying to versify my Dream about the "Spectre Drummer," with the shroud flying over his shoulders; and to introduce it in a new poem, which will be as wild and horrible as Golgotha; but "I loves to make people afraid" ' " (Beattie, 1:504). The letter is dated January 18, 1809, as he was completing "Gertrude," but "The Spectre Boat" was not published until 1822, when he included it in the *New Monthly*.

In "The Turkish Lady," Campbell used the oriental theme that fascinated so many Englishmen of his day, but this poem is a slight sentimental romance telling of a Turkish lady's falling in love with a captive English knight and eloping with him to Rhodes, where "the British lover / Clasp'd his blooming Eastern bride" (ll. 39–40). Campbell began the poem in 1800, while he was in Germany anticipating a trip to the lower part of Hungary; he completed it at Sydenham in 1804.

His trip to Germany in 1820 inspired "The Brave Roland," a story of unrequited love set in the romantic scenery of the Rhine River, where an ancient tower, the Rolandseck, was supposedly built by the great warrior-hero Roland within view of a nunnery to which his beloved had gone after hearing the false news of his death. A Mrs. Arkwright set the poem to music for young ladies to sing.

Two more short legendary poems, both printed in the *New Monthly* in 1822, celebrate the return of a lover from afar. In "Adelgitha," the lover acts as a deus ex machina, a champion in disguise to rescue the condemned Adelgitha as the "fatal trumpet sounded" and then to reveal himself as "her own true knight" to whom she has been faithful. "Song," beginning "Earl March looked on his dying child," is likewise sentimental. The earl summons home a youth, whom he had earlier exiled, to woo his child, now dying from grief or from disease (not clear). After long anticipating his return, she dies anyway of a broken heart when he fails to recognize her pale and wasted face. Campbell's is a variant of the same theme Scott had used in "The Maid of Neidpath." Such poems, according to Hill, "testify in favour of the growing opinion, that poetry (despite John Milton) if intended to maintain a permanent hold upon a nation's affectionate sympathies, must be short, terse, nervous, and graphic, and will produce the most lasting effects if conveyed to the mind, through the ear, with the addition of melody of sound and rhythm."[12]

CHAPTER 5

"Fanciful Convictions": The Miscellaneous Poems

C AMPBELL'S remaining work includes forty-nine titles that Robertson calls "Miscellaneous Poems," besides "Songs, Chiefly Amatory," "Translations, Chiefly from the Greek," and "Juvenilia." Many of them are only slight occasional pieces, such as "To the Infant Son of my dear friends, Mr. and Mrs. Grahame," or "To a Young Lady who asked me to write something original for her Album." These and other complimentary verses, written to fulfill expectations from a "bard," are hardly worth noticing, and space prohibits attention to the translations and juvenilia.

Some of the poems in the "Miscellaneous" group are among Campbell's best efforts, and the collection reveals the major themes in his poetry. These include faith, sometimes in conflict with doubt; nostalgia and a longing for the Golden Age; a visionary sense of nature and man's relation to it; the lure of the unknown; human suffering and endurance, especially by women; alienation and separation; love and friendship; transitoriness; and the archetypes, both characters and themes. The variety of these poems which express the human emotions and delight the human spirit, makes clear Campbell's versatility.

Today the one most frequently read of the miscellaneous poems is "The Last Man," treating a scientific-religious theme of human faith that still appeals to the imagination. The poet-narrator explains that he has had a vision in his sleep of the last days of the Creation. In his dream, he saw the last human survivor of all the wars, plagues, and famines of earth dauntlessly addressing the fading sun in the role of a prophet. " 'We are twins in death, proud Sun!' " (l. 25). Continuing to speak for the remaining three-fourths of the poem, the man welcomes the end, stating pessimistically that all of his race's

103

accomplishments " 'healed not a passion or a pang / Entailed on human hearts' " (ll. 39–40). Although he anticipates the death of worldly things, he expects to outlive the sun in the brighter bliss of heaven. As the last of Adam's race, he tells the sun to tell the night that he heroically defies the " 'darkening universe . . . / To quench his immortality / Or shake his trust in God!' " (ll. 79–80). He will be reunited with the spiritual power from which he originated.

In this poem, Campbell harks back to the Calvinistic doctrines of his father. The work is an eschatological vision in the traditional Chistian sense; it also completes the pattern of the rebirth archetype left unfinished in poems like "The Spectre-Boat" and "The Death-Boat of Heligoland," which end with punishment or the night-journey. In addition, it follows logically the conclusion to "The Pleasures of Hope," where Hope survives "Nature's funeral pile."

In writing "The Last Man" for inclusion in the *New Monthly Magazine* in 1823, Campbell was using a popular theme. Some of his predecessors, aside from sermon writers, were Coleridge, whose "Rime of the Ancient Mariner" (1798) is one version; a French priest named Grainville, who published a poem, "Le Dernier Homme," in 1804; the anonymous writer of the novel *The Last Man or Omegarius and Sideria, a Romance in Futurity* (1806); Shelley, who held a conversation with Byron on the subject before Byron's "Darkness" appeared in 1816; Byron; and even Cyrus Redding, who says that as a youth in 1811 he printed a little poem that contained a last-man passage. When Thomas Lovell Beddoes projected a drama on the topic, his friend Barry Cornwall (Bryan Waller Procter), reported the fact to Campbell, thereby spurring Campbell to complete his poem. Beddoes' efforts, however, remain only fragments composed between 1823 and 1825; Mary W. Shelley wrote her novel *The Last Man* in 1826; and Thomas Hood composed a burlesque poem of the same title, also in 1826.

Campbell's sensitivity to charges of plagiarism provoked him to write to his cousin William Gray on September 5, 1823, shortly after the poem was published: " 'Did you see "The Last Man" in my late number? Did it immediately remind you of Lord Byron's poem of "Darkness"? I was a little troubled how to act about this appearance of my having been obliged to him for the idea.' " He goes on to state that, if anything, Byron borrowed from him: " 'The fact is, many years ago I had the idea of this Last Man in my head, and distinctly remember speaking of the subject to Lord B. I recognised, when I read his poem "Darkness," some traits of the picture which I meant to draw, namely, the ships floating without living hands to guide them—the earth being blank—and one or two more circumstances.' " Yet he will not accuse Byron. " 'It is consistent with my own experience to suppose that an idea, which is actually one of memory, may start up, appearing to be one of the imagination, in a mind that has forgot the source from which it borrowed that idea. I believe this.' " Neither did he wish to attach a note to his poem which " 'would have had the appearance of picking a quarrel with the noble bard.' " Besides, " 'the likeness of our subjects does not seem to strike any reader of my poem so much as I expected; so that, unless charged with plagiarism, I may let the matter rest' " (Beattie, 2:154).

As it turned out, he was accused of borrowing by his friend Jeffrey of the *Edinburgh Review,* who compared the two poems: "Lord Byron's has more variety of topics, more gloom and terror, and far more daring and misanthropy. Mr. Campbell's has more sweetness, more reflection, more considerate loftiness, and more of the spirit of religion."[1]

Even a friendly accusation was too much for Campbell to leave unanswered. He sent a letter of explanation addressed "To the Editor of the Edinburgh Review" to the *Times,* where it appeared March 24, 1825, and thereafter in other periodicals and papers (but not in the *Edinburgh Review*).[2] Campbell's protestations provided an opportunity for satire by writers of the *London Magazine,* who could not resist laughing at him for charging Byron with using what was really only a commonplace idea and for blaming others for plagiarizing what he was only contemplating.[3] The last word on the controversy is Redding's comment on the use of archetypal themes in literature: "Such are sometimes the errors of literary men as to originality. How many have related the same waking visions, and how many of those whose dust now nourishes the food for our sustenance repeated those of their ancestors."[4]

The next year, 1824, Campbell published another visionary poem, "A Dream" about himself. He begins by establishing the relation between reality and fantasy:

> Well may sleep present us fictions,
>   Since our waking moments teem
> With such fanciful convictions
>   As make life itself a dream.

Moving then to a specific example, the poet recounts his very realistic "dream of yesternight." The vision was of another spectre-boat cast on the "sea of life," and he was steering it himself, alone, experiencing "sad regrets from past existence" (l. 19) while "shadowed in the forward distance / Lay the land of death" (ll. 21–22). "On that dim-seen shore" he beheld two hands "unshroud a spectre's face" (l. 26)—his own. Suddenly the ocean kindled "like an emerald spark," and "an air-dropt being / Smiling steered my bark" (ll. 31–32). He was "heaven-like," but human in appearance with "supernal beauty," "more compassionate than woman," and "lordly more than man." At this heavenly being's behest Campbell, like a soldier scorning death in response to "some sweet clarion's breath" (l. 37), brooked "the spectre's eyes of icy look, / Till it shut them, turned its head / Like a beaten foe, and fled" (ll. 40–42). Interpreting this victory to mean that his "death-hour" was not yet come, the poet asked his guardian spirit to tell him his future. The wise spirit refused to grant him such a curse; neither would he yield to the other request he sensed " 'revolving in . . . [his protégé's] breast' ": " 'to live again, . . . / In thy second life-time treasuring / Knowledge from the first' " (ll. 56–60). The spirit chided him as a " 'poor self-deceiver' " if he should wish the " 'fitful fever' " of " 'life's career . . . new begun again.' " Whatever governs life, whether fate (the predestination of Campbell's rejected Calvinism) or chance, the spirit pointed out that experience ten times over could not keep " 'pain from being' " or avoid " 'heaven's lightning' "; " 'nor could thy foresight's glance / 'Scape the myriad shafts of chance' " (ll. 69–70). Besides, who would wish to " 'bear again love's trouble' " and " 'friendship's death dissevered ties,' " or to " 'toil to grasp or miss the bubble / Of ambition's prize?' " (ll. 71–74). The spirit continues:

> "Say thy life's new guided action
>   Flowed from virtue's fairest springs—
> Still would envy and detraction
>   Double not their stings?" (ll. 75–78).

Then the poet, having caught the moral, urged the spirit to steer him on, " 'Envying, fearing, hating none ' " (l. 83).

Beattie compares "A Dream" with "The Last Man" (1823), judging "A Dream" "worthy of its predecessor, . . . which it much resembles, but does not reach, either in poetical conception or expression" (2:164). The two poems resemble each other in that both are dream visions, both contain beings able to prophesy, and both end with an affirmative religious note: man accepting bravely his assigned course. The last man knows his destiny; the dreamer lives in faith. Both are heroic, and both hold out the lure of the unknown.

"A Dream" also reflects some kinship with Shelley's "Alastor" (1816), especially in the part where the lonely young poet-wanderer flees in his hegira to meet death on the deep, and his boat is driven over the sea, into a cave, and out again into a calm cove. Both poets use ancient Odyssean themes with variations. Both express an experience potentially common to all—a night journey leading to rebirth and renewal.

In "A Dream," according to Beattie, "there is throughout a marked allusion to his [Campbell's] own private fortunes in the race of life" (2:164). At the time, 1824, the year of his son's illness, his wife's poor health, and his own intermittent sickness and sleeplessness, Campbell verbalized some of his emotional dilemmas in his poetry, which may have afforded him cathartic therapy with its restatement of traditional religious values. "Reullura" and "The Ritter Bann" both came out that year also, and Beattie notes that the manuscripts of all three lyrics were much revised before publication (2:164). Both "Reullura" and "The Ritter Bann" portray heroic, faithful wives. "Theodric," Campbell's "*domestic* and private story" with its two faithful heroines, likewise appeared in 1824. "The Spectre-Boat," the 1822 ballad that "A Dream" resembles, ends with the religious note of punishment for faithless wrongdoing. It contains no personal vision, however, except the possible dramatization of a guilty conscience.

An 1819 poem, "To the Rainbow," has a renewal theme and devotional feeling. Campbell published it in the *New Monthly* in January 1821 and in the *Theodric* volume in 1824. Along with "The Last Man," it was a popular success; according to W. A. Hill: "Few pieces of poetry in the English language, if we except the 'Advent Hymn' and the 'Star in the East,' verses rejected by Campbell from his printed poems, have been more frequently called upon to do duty (without leave) in the pages of complimentary editions of religious hymn-books of all kinds than the 'Rainbow' and the 'Last Man.' " The Reverend Mr. Hill considers such borrowing "a valuable testimony . . not only to the beauty and sweetness of their composition, but to the sound religious and devotional feeling operative in the mind of their author."[5]

The conflicts in "To the Rainbow" are between scientific fact and religious faith or between "cold material laws" and "the poet's theme." Addressing the "triumphal arch," the poet-speaker refutes any need for "proud Philosophy" or Newton's *Opticks* to teach him what a rainbow is. To him as a child it was an archetypal bridge: "A midway station given / For happy spirits to alight / Betwixt the earth and heaven" (ll. 6–8). Another pleasant childhood dream was that "of gems and gold / Hid in thy radiant bow" (ll. 11–12). Now,

> When Science from Creation's face
>   Enchantment's veil withdraws,
> What lovely visions yield their place
>   To cold material laws! (ll. 13–16)

Why the rainbow exists as "Heaven's covenant" is explained in "words of the Most High." The rainbow likely inspired "the first man-made anthem" and the first poet's song.

> Nor ever shall the Muse's eye
>   Unraptured greet thy beam:
> Theme of primeval prophecy,
>   Be still the poet's theme! (ll. 33–36)

A rainbow is always welcomed and always looks fresh and young,

> For, faithful to its sacred page,
>   Heaven still rebuilds thy span,
> Nor lets the type grow pale with age
>   That first spoke peace to man (ll. 49–52).

Shelley's "The Cloud" (1820) similarly treats rebuilding and cyclical renewal.

A writer for *Blackwood's* who signed himself "Detector" accused Campbell of plagiarizing "The Rainbow" of Henry Vaughan, whom he had treated with derogation in *Specimens of the British Poets*. The "world's grey fathers" is used in both poems as an epithet for the early watchers of the rainbow. "Detector" thought "The Last Man" and Byron's "Darkness" were too unlike for any charge of plagiarism, but he felt Campbell here should have given credit to Vaughan.[6]

Although "The Rainbow," according to Hill, in its final version is materially different from the original publication, its thirteen quatrains could be reduced. As it is, it is too long to support its theme without monotony. Stanzas 7, 10, and 11, for example, contain irrelevant scenes that Campbell evidently liked too well to cut. Even so, they affirm the appeal of the rainbow to the human spirit.

In 1825, Campbell attempted a poem on a difficult subject—the definition of "Hallowed Ground." For sixteen rather obscure stanzas he rejects various possibilities—cemeteries, churches, spots hallowed by individual associations, monuments, and trophies. Instead, he finds hallowed ground intangible: "To live in hearts we leave behind, / Is not to die" (ll. 35–36), and "The heart alone can make divine / Religion's spot" (ll. 59–60). The final answer is that hallowed ground is "what gives birth / To sacred thoughts in souls of worth!" (ll. 91–92). The "high priesthood" of Peace, Independence, and Truth will make "earth / All hallow'd ground!" (ll. 95–96). In this poem Campbell thus rejects all forms of superstition in advocacy of spiritual freedom, but the poem is not a very satisfactory one.

During his first year as lord rector of the University of Glasgow, 1826, Campbell wrote his "Lines on Revisiting a Scottish River." Its four Spenserian stanzas express a nostalgic longing for the Eden of his youth forty years before and make a scathing indictment of modern industrialism. Hypocritical "improvements" have ruined the environment and taken a high human toll, as Campbell the ecologist cries out:

> And call they this improvement?—to have changed,
> My native Clyde, thy once romantic shore,
> Where nature's face is banished and estranged,
> And heaven reflected in thy wave no more;
> Whose banks, that sweetened May-day's breath before,
> Lie sere and leafless now in summer's beam,
> With sooty exhalations covered o'er;
> And for the daisied greensward, down thy stream
> Unsightly brick-lanes smoke and clanking engines gleam (ll. 1–9).

(In this last line the sound perfectly echoes the sense.) To Campbell, "One heart free tasting nature's breath and bloom / Is worth a thousand slaves to mammon's gains" (ll. 11–12). He wonders where the wealth goes, and whom it gladdens. As Goldsmith might have said, "To gorge a few with trade's precarious prize / We banish rural life, and breathe unwholesome skies" (ll. 26–27).

The Glasgow Campbell describes is still the Glasgow of today in those parts

> . . . where the human breed
> Degenerates as they swarm and overflow,
> Till toil grows cheaper than the trodden weed,
> And man competes with man, like foe with foe,
> Till death, that thins them, scarce seems public woe (ll. 19–23).

People are "left but life enough and breathing-room / The hunger and the hope of life to feel" (ll. 14–15). Such an evil is not slight, "For not alone our frame imbibes a stain / From foetid skies—the spirit's healthy pride / Fades in their gloom" (ll. 32–34). Campbell shows here that he understood well the sociological problems of the slums and their effects on the quality of human life.

Another sociological poem of this period is "Lines on the Departure of Emigrants for New South Wales" (1828). In it Campbell depicts very sensitively the feelings of the "pensive band" he saw leaving for "earth's remotest strand," Australia. Their grief at departure from "the home that could not yield them bread" (l. 4) is very real, like that of "children parting from a mother" (l. 3), and their homesickness will cause them to give "England's names to distant scenes" (l. 13). Gradually, however, their new abode will become an earthly paradise, a place of freedom, opportunity, and abundance in which their children will take pride. The one hundred twenty-two lines of the poem capture something of the lure of the unknown:

> These are the hopes, high-minded hopes and strong,
> That beckon England's wanderers o'er the brine
> To realms where foreign constellations shine,
> Where streams from undiscovered fountains roll,
> And winds shall fan them from th' Antarctic pole (ll. 30–34).

One idyllic scene Campbell envisions—a child twining "his tame young kangaroo with flowers" (l. 114)—became one of the vignettes in later illustrated editions of his poems. Still later, an Australian writer chose "Kangaroo with Flowers" as his title for an article expressing appreciation for Campbell's role in influencing the attitudes and hopes of the colonists, and urging his inclusion in the canon of Australian literature.[7]

A similar encouragement for another group of settlers is "Song of the Colonists Departing for New Zealand." These peaceful heroes can sing a chorus that goes:

> Cheer up! cheer up! our course we'll keep
>   With dauntless heart and hand;
> And when we've ploughed the stormy deep,
>   We'll plough a smiling land (ll. 5–8).

All of his life Campbell sympathized with exiles and alienated persons. When he himself was abroad in 1800 and feeling what it was like to be away from one's homeland, his heart went out to the young Anthony MacCann, who had been exiled for his role on the side of the United Irishmen in the Irish Rebellion of 1798.[8] His response to MacCann's plight inspired the sentimental "Exile of Erin," in which the pathetic exile is sighing for his country at twilight, bewailing his fate that "a home and a country remain not to me" (l. 12), wondering about his family, and still giving his blessing to the "sweetest isle of the ocean" (l. 38): "Erin go bragh!"[9]

Campbell wrote the five-stanza poem shortly after reaching Germany and sent it home to Perry, who printed it in the *Morning Chronicle* on January 28, 1801, with a preface urging parliamentary benevolence for such men. Translated into German and also set to music, the song solaced the exiles themselves and appealed to the emotions of a wide audience back home.[10] Such common property did the poem become that others even claimed its authorship, causing Campbell and his friends to have to defend his rights.

During his stay in Germany, Campbell voiced his own sense of alienation in several poems. "Lines Written on Visiting a Scene in Argyleshire" he began in 1798 but finished in 1800 in Hamburg and sent home for inclusion in the *Morning Chronicle*. The "scene" is the ruined home of his forefathers, Kirnan, in the vale of Glassary, last inhabited by his grandfather, Archibald Campbell. During his nostalgic visit, Campbell had found "One rose of the wilderness left on its stalk / To mark where a garden had been" (ll. 12–13). This rose, "the last of its race" (l. 14), became the "emblem of all / That remains in this desolate heart!" (ll. 19–20). Not only for the social status of his forefathers and his own departed boyhood does the young man long, but also for a lost love (his "Caroline"). "Though the wilds of enchantment . . . Abandon my soul like a dream of the night / And leave but a desert behind" (ll. 23–27), he feels that "to bear is to conquer our fate" (l. 36). The poem succeeds well in conveying the feeling of loneliness and determined endurance he dramatized later in "The Last Man."

In "Lines on Leaving a Scene in Bavaria" (1800), Campbell combined his enthusiasm for the unspoiled scenery of the Danube with a profound sense of estrangement that struck a responsive chord in Byron, who called the poem "perfectly magnificent."[11] Campbell's passages of feeling that Byron liked to the point of echoing in his own poetry include: "Roll on, ye mighty waters, roll! / And rage, thou darkened sky!" (ll. 17–18). Childe Harold would agree that "to him who flies from many woes / Even homeless deserts can be dear!" (ll. 48–49). The poem ends with the mood Byron later made famous:

> No longer wish, no more repine
> For man's neglect or woman's scorn;
> Then wed thee to an exile's lot,
> For, if the world hath loved thee not,
> Its absence may be borne (ll. 149–53).

Campbell says his farewell to Bavaria during the autumn season, an appropriate time to contrast his present feelings with his own past spring. The solitude of the wild romantic scene matches his mood of withdrawn isolation and his desire to escape. The lines seem to have been composed over a period of time, however, and then imperfectly unified. The coherence of the seventeen nine-line stanzas is hard to follow, as is the syntax of the sentences. Hadden is correct: "The lines certainly bear traces of genuine feeling, but the piece as a whole is obscure and unfinished."[12]

At the close of 1800, when he himself was suffering from the "favour" of Judith, Campbell wrote his "Ode to Winter," in which he was able to objectify his feelings. He begins by personifying the four seasons as children of the sun. Spring and fall, and especially summer, pay homage to their sire, but "howling Winter" flees afar to Scandinavian darkness. Then the poet sentimentally prays the "sire of storms" and "power of desolation" that he will rule gently, not "chill the wanderer's bosom bare" or "freeze the wretch's falling tear" (ll. 43–44).

> To shuddering Want's unmantled bed
> Thy horror-breathing agues cease to lend,
> And gently on the orphan head
> Of innocence descend (ll. 45–48).

A special concern is "The sailor on his airy shrouds / When wrecks and beacons strew the steep, / And spectres walk along the deep" (ll.

50–52)—an image Campbell was fond of repeating. The poem ends with an intercession for the soldiers tented along the Rhine and the Danube. Even though the fallen are spared by winter's "unhallowed breath," "man will ask no truce to death, / No bounds to human woe" (ll. 63–64). Savage nature is less fearful than savage human nature.

About this time, or in January 1801, came "Lines on the Grave of a Suicide," originally entitled "Lines written on seeing the unclaimed corpse of a suicide exposed on the banks of a river." Campbell's natural sympathy for a suicide was doubled by the dead man's being "By strangers left upon a lonely shore, / Unknown, unhonoured, . . . friendless" (ll. 1–2). Even the superstitious fishermen will avoid the area, afraid to meet the "poor unfortunate." The poet asks: "Who may understand / Thy many woes, poor suicide, unknown?" (ll. 18–19). The conclusion is that "he who thy being gave shall judge of thee alone" (l. 20), the "alone" repeating the "lonely" of the first line to sound the complete isolation of the victim.

A much less serious poem of 1800, "The Beech-Tree's Petition," shows Campbell's playful concern for a large beech tree that was about to become the victim of a gardener who proposed to cut it down because no crop would grow near it and it had no business being in a kitchen garden. As a somewhat sentimental ecologist, the poet has the tree speak its own petition, arguing for the esthetic values of love and beauty as opposed to utilitarian uses. Campbell wrote the short poem at the request of his sister Mary, who was a friend to the ladies championing the tree. Its owner, evidently more out of deference to the ladies than to Campbell's poem at first, spared the tree. Later the man took pride in being the proprietor of the famous beech and recounted its story to Scott and to Beattie (1:276–78).

Campbell's sympathy with suffering and his championship of justice inspired his "Love and Madness, an Elegy," which he completed in 1796 at the age of nineteen. Originally entitled "Monody on Miss Broderick," the poem is a study of the love-hate relationship in the form of a dramatic monologue spoken by a Miss Broderick, then in prison for murder. In a letter to James Thomson from Downie in Argyllshire, September 15, 1796, Campbell explains the background:

The subject is the unhappy fair one, who, you may remember, was tried about twelve months ago for the murder of Errington. Some of my critical friends have blamed me for endeavoring to recommend such a woman to sympathy; but from the moment I heard Broderick's story, I could not refrain from admiring her, even amid the horror of the rash deed she committed.

Errington was an inhuman villain to forsake her, and he deserved his fate; not by the laws of his country, but of friendship, which he had so heinously broken through (Beattie, 1:150).

In this Gothic poem, his earliest treatment of a woman triumphing over a faithless man, he imagines that the tolling of the midnight bell in Warwick Castle has aroused "Poor Broderick," who "wakes—in solitude to weep." The "friendless mourner" can hardly endure her "pensive thoughts . . . of Fortune's better day" (ll. 7–8). She sighs Errington's "melancholy name," hears his spirit wailing in every storm, and "in midnight shades" views his "passing form." As she relives the murder, she bespeaks pity for herself and condemns smugness in those "proud fair" who have never experienced the anguish of "perjured pride's inhuman scorn." Because Errington's "sleepless spirit, breathing from the tomb, / Foretells my fate, and summons me to come!" (ll. 63–64) she longs for "the dreamless night of long repose" (l. 70) and "the bourne / Where, lulled to slumber, grief forgets to mourn!" (ll. 71–72).

"The 'Name Unknown' " (1800), a graceful imitation of Klopstock's "Ode to His Future Love," is both a compliment to Klopstock, whom Campbell met at this time, and a speculation on the name of his own future mate, whom he envisions as a guardian angel "ordained to bless my charmèd soul, / And all my future fate control, / Unrivalled and alone" (ll. 4–6).

Occasionally Campbell used his verbal gifts to pay tribute to the memory of famous people, thereby vicariously enriching himself through the relationship. "Ode to the Memory of Burns" (1815) is one such poem. In it Campbell expresses his admiration for the widely loved Burns, to whom "love's own strain . . . was given" (l. 13), who taught "patriot-pride" and "the inborn worth of man," and beneath whose touch "rustic life and poverty / Grew beautiful" (ll. 27–30). The penultimate stanza best epitomizes his great compatriot:

> Farewell, high chief of Scottish song!
> That couldst alternately impart
> Wisdom and rapture in thy page,
> And brand each vice with satire strong—
> Whose lines are mottoes of the heart,
> Whose truths electrify the sage (ll. 79–84).[13]

He also uses two stanzas to state the case for poetry, which is not "an idle art." The poet is he who "refines . . . / The nobler passions of the soul" (ll. 59–60), and whose muse "consecrates / The native banner of the brave, / Unfurling at the trumpet's breath / Rose, thistle, harp . . ." (ll. 61–64). Additionally in this multipurpose poem comes Campbell's feeling for exiles and expatriates, for Burns's poems can solace "the Scottish exile," who can

> Bend o'er his home-born verse, and weep
> In memory of his native land,
> With love that scorns the lapse of time,
> And ties that stretch beyond the deep (ll. 45–48).

When John P. Kemble retired from the stage, Campbell, who had known him for fifteen years, composed seven "Valedictory Stanzas" to be read at a public festival in his honor on June 27, 1817. Kemble, a popular tragic actor and one-time manager of the Drury Lane Theatre, was brother to Mrs. Sarah Kemble Siddons, with whom he sometimes performed. In paying tribute to the numerous roles he had played, Campbell called him the "pride of the British stage, . . . Whose image brought the heroic age / Revived to Fancy's view" (ll. 1–4). Then he eulogized the theater arts, comparing acting with poetry, painting, and sculpture. Acting is "the youngest of the sister Arts, / Where all their beauty blends" (ll. 15–16). For slighting poetry, Campbell's muse did not put forth her best effort, but the *Spectator* complimented the poem, to Campbell's great pleasure, and Kemble appreciated it. It sounds like an artificially wordy declamation, but Campbell was well satisfied with it.

A number of Campbell's poems have the unimaginative titles, "Lines on . . . ," and unstructured lines often tend toward such wordiness as that in "Lines on the View from St. Leonards." Because, like Byron, Campbell responded emotionally to the sea and frequently went to the coast for periods of restoration, it was inevitable that he should write about the ocean. This poem, containing several echoes of "Childe Harold's Pilgrimage," is the result of one such visit in 1831. The subject proved vaster than Campbell's ability, despite the one hundred thirty-six lines of blank verse he attempted, but he did write some good lines communicating his feelings and describing the sea, both displaying "chameleon-like" moods. The poem opens with his statement of appreciation:

> Hail to thy face and odours, glorious Sea!
> 'Twere thanklessness in me to bless thee not,
> Great beauteous Being! in whose breath and smile

My heart beats calmer, and my very mind
Inhales salubrious thoughts. How welcomer
Thy murmurs than the murmurs of the world!
Though like the world thou fluctuat'st, thy din
To me is peace, thy restlessness repose (ll. 1–8).

The sea can "reach / The inmost immaterial mind's recess, / And . . . stir its chords / To music" (ll. 64–67). This archetypal concept, which accounts for man's response to the ocean, Campbell states in lines with Wordsworthian echoes:

The Spirit of the Universe in thee
Is visible; thou hast in thee the life—
The eternal, graceful, and majestic life—
Of nature, and the natural human heart
Is therefore bound to thee with holy love (ll. 68–72).

Mother-sea is timeless, eternal, not subject to death;

But long as Man to parent Nature owns
Instinctive homage, and in times beyond
The power of thought to reach, bard after bard
Shall sing thy glory, beatific Sea! (ll. 133–36)

Campbell thought this poem one of his best.

During his last years, other aspects of nature, especially the strong ones like the ocean, inspired Campbell's muse and served as vicarious compensation for his own physical weakness. "Ben Lomond" (1836) contrasts the steadfastness of the mountain, "white-headed Ben," with the mortality of man. "Cora Linn, or the Falls of Clyde" opposes the calm of the glen to the noise of the linn (waterfall); then it contrasts romantic Cora with Niagara, "king of all" but a noisy "barbarian" that "appals the wilderness."[14] "The Dead Eagle," written in Algiers in 1835, celebrates the "natural strength and power" of "the bird of Jove" that, even fallen, "still seems / Like royalty in ruins" (ll. 1–2). Then, in the same rambling blank verse poem, Campbell changes his subject to a lion, using as his transition the statement, "Strange is the imagination's dread delight / In objects linked with danger, death, and pain!" (ll. 77–78). His heart, he says, "beat with joy when first I heard / A lion's roar come down the Libyan wind / Across yon long, wide, lonely inland lake" (ll. 81–83).

"A Thought Suggested by the New Year," published in the *New*

Monthly Magazine in February 1836, uses an ironic *tempus fugit* theme to contrast the rapid passage of time in sorrowful and vapid old age with the lingering "current of our youth, / Ere passion yet disorders" (ll. 5–6). With fortunate justice, heaven's gift to "our years of fading strength" is "indemnifying fleetness," whereas to "those of youth a seeming length, / Proportion'd to their sweetness" (ll. 23–24). The feminine rhymes of the second and fourth lines of each stanza give the impression of movement.

In his lifetime of miscellaneous poetry, Campbell composed some satire and humorous verse, which were seldom successful. The examples that survive prove why he chose to publish little of such in his collected works. Among the poems that Robertson groups as "Songs, Chiefly Amatory" are two drinking songs, gracefully done, with such sentiments as "drink to her that each loves most / As she would love to hear" (ll. 11–12). This one, entitled merely "Song," Campbell published in the *New Monthly* in 1822. The other is "Drinking-Song of Munich," translated from the German in 1800. It exalts the "golden flagons," "for wine can triumph over woe" (l. 17).

Many of the lady loves of Campbell's life figure in his amatory poems, but most of these poems are about the idea of love rather than expressions of love itself—again, a hopeless hope. To his friend Caroline on the Isle of Mull he addressed two poems—"Part I: To the South Wind" in 1795 and "Part II: To the Evening Star" in 1796. Both are the kind of compliment a young classics scholar would pay a lady. "To Judith" (Altona, 1800) expresses a longing for the pastoral simplicity of "Judah's happy clime" where "I had fed thy father's flocks, / . . . To win thee to my arms" (ll. 8–10); instead, Judah now is "a desert and a tomb!" His future wife Matilda was the subject of "Ode to Content," also written at the end of 1800. To the "cherub Content" he says: "I would pay all my vows if Matilda were mine" (l. 14); but the smile of Matilda's favor seems short:

> In the pulse of my heart I have nourished a care
> Which forbids me thy sweet inspiration to share;
> The noon of my youth slow departing I see,
> But its years, as they roll, bring no tidings of thee (ll. 9–12).

In "Absence," printed in the *New Monthly* in 1821, he says that separation tears the soul "From more than light, or life, or breath" (l. 14). It is "the pain without the peace of death!" (l. 16).

In 1821 also he printed "The Lover to His Mistress on Her

Birthday," subtitled "A Song Translated from the Bohemian." Its tone is definitely more erotic than some:

> I gazed, and felt upon my lips
>   The unfinished accents hang:
> One moment's bliss, one burning kiss,
>   To rapture changed each pang (ll. 13–16).

The speaker recollects:

> And, though as swift as lightning's flash
>   Those trancèd moments flew,
> Not all the waves of time shall wash
>   Their memory from my view (ll. 17–20).

Another "Song" in the *New Monthly,* in 1823, expresses a similar *tempus fugit* theme, with the first of its two stanzas reading:

> Withdraw not yet those lips and fingers,
>   Whose touch to mine is rapture's spell;
> Life's joy for us a moment lingers,
>   And death seems in the word—farewell.
> The hour that bids us part and go,
> It sounds not yet,—oh! no, no, no!

In 1830, about the time his rumored second marriage came to naught, Campbell bade "Farewell to Love," saying,

> I've known, if ever mortal knew, the spells of Beauty's thrall,
> And, if my song has told them not, my soul has felt them all;
> But Passion robs my peace no more, and Beauty's witching sway
> Is now to me a star that's fallen—a dream that's passed away (ll. 5–8).

No doubt Campbell enjoyed writing his amatory verses, and certainly they served as an emotional outlet for him. In them he often expressed the tensions between feeling and logic, between the pleasure and the transience of life. In doing so he gave words to experiences potentially common to all persons.

CHAPTER 6

The Booksellers' Slave: The Prose Works

C AMPBELL'S prose increased his income more than it did his fame. All of his life he chose to write for the booksellers and the periodicals to meet his mundane needs, not from the inspiration of his muse. Otherwise he found his income insufficient, and writing was the only profession he had. For him, prose composition was an onerous kind of manufacture in which he took little joy. Fortunately, the current practice of anonymity helped him protect his identity in publishing much of it. In a letter that Beattie quotes, Campbell complains of " 'this perpetual galley-slavery, which will for ever debar me from the only consolation of my existence—that of writing, or attempting to write, poetry. I see no hope of rescue from unprofitable drudgery' " (1:529).

I   Annals of Great Britain

On October 30, 1802, Campbell wrote to Lord Minto that he had been "supplying an Edinburgh bookseller with anonymous and, consequently, inglorious articles in prose—a labor, in fact, little superior to compilation, and more connected with profit than reputation." He adds: "In this literary fagging, and in editing an edition of some Greek tragedies, which Mundell means to publish, I shall probably be confined eight or nine hours a day during the winter. As to Poetry, I believe I have lost both the faculty and the inclination for writing it" (Beattie, 1:331). At that time, he was having trouble completing and revising the poems he had already begun. Beattie adds that the anonymous prose work here referred to was the *Annals of Great Britain*, to be done in three volumes octavo for a hundred pounds per volume (p. 332), but he does not explain the edition of the tragedies.

Campbell wrote again to Minto, December 27, 1802, that he had engaged to do a "historical work, intended as a continuation of Smollett's down to the present time." The small compensation he was to receive was not "sufficient to tempt me to put my name to it. It is not to be written for reputation, but for employment, and as a trial of my hand at a new species of literary labor." In seeking permission from Minto to quote some of his parliamentary speeches, he explained his attitude toward the project:

Although I do not come like a trembling culprit before the public, I feel interested, even to enthusiasm, in my new undertaking; and shall, perhaps, write with more spirit, than if I set to it with the embarrassing impression of the public looking over my shoulder. Public events for fifty years past, have followed in pretty interesting succession; and I should think the man's heart very listless indeed, who could sit down to relate and review them without strong animation. Whatever my history may turn out—and possibly it may prove both dull and dry—I shall begin it, at least, with the favorable omens of zeal and interest—anonymous although I mean it to be (Beattie, 1:336).

Beattie comments that Campbell was so apprehensive of "losing *caste*, by descending from the province of lofty rhyme, to that of mere historical compilation, that 'he bound his employers to secrecy, and did not wish the fact to be known even amongst his intimate friends' " (p. 338).

Later, in a letter to one close friend, John Richardson, on July 14, 1804, Campbell explained that at the time he was courting his wife he had entered into an agreement for a "History of England." "The bargain was that I was to do it plainly and decently—but, as the price they could afford was but small, it was to be *anonymous.*" Now, with the book nearly finished, he was having some difficulties with the publishers that Richardson could help settle. Fearing they might even throw the book back onto his hands, Campbell complained: " 'I have no objections to do journeyman's work, yet I don't wish to be congratulated by all the world on the appearance of my History!' " (Beattie, 1:399–400).

In November 1804, he was looking forward to its completion and the opportunity to write something more congenial. Because he was occasionally sidetracked to other more lucrative jobs, however, the *Annals of Great Britain from the Ascension* [Accession] *of George IIId. to the Peace of Amiens* did not appear until 1807, published by Constable in three volumes. It did not attract critical notice until 1809.

The *Monthly Review* began with an appreciation of the author's decision to publish his volumes "in the unambitious shape of Annals, and to forego all claims to the reputation of a finished history" because of the difficulty of obtaining authentic documents for so recent a period of history, in which "the principal actors or their immediate descendants are alive, and liable to be affected."[1] The reviewer, Joseph Lowe, a businessman and writer, pointed out that the simple narrative, in forty chapters not subdivided into coherent sections, has a number of merits, including the author's descriptive powers and his ability to report with "condensed and animated statement" (p. 361) both sides of parliamentary debates. Yet it also contains many careless errors in typography and style, indicating haste and a lack of proofreading and revision. "The author of this book is better qualified for emphatic delineation than laborious research," said Lowe, and he recommended that if he should attempt to write history again, he ought to "keep this distinction in view in making choice of his subject." At the least, "His intentions appear to be irreproachable; he is always the advocate of liberality; and his errors never bear the stamp of wilful misrepresentation" (p. 365). Despite Campbell's precautions, Lowe ended: "Report has assigned this production to the pen of Mr. Campbell, author of the 'Pleasures of Hope,' and, alas! of 'Gertrude of Wyoming' " (p. 366).

The *British Critic* got around to reviewing the *Annals* a year later, expressing embarrassment that the work had escaped its notice for three years. The reviewer found the volumes "no less interesting, and certainly much more candid, than *some* of the *histories* of the same period," but he noted at the outset that "the author is indeed a *Whig*."[2] Regardless of some wrong opinions (in the reviewer's judgment) and some unproved assertions, "his detail of events is generally luminous and faithful; and in support of his party he is never rancorous" (p. 250). In the work "this annalist" advocates licentiousness instead of just liberty of the press, attacks required subscription to the thirty-nine articles of the Church of England, talks "of the violation of the natural and chartered rights of the [American] colonies" (p. 257), lauds Charles James Fox, and misstates, out of party prejudice, the popular reaction to the Pitt and Grenville acts (the sedition and treason acts). In his favor, however, is his impartiality in tracing "the rise and progress of the French Revolution" (p. 335).

The style is "on the whole good," but there are occasional errors in usage, such as "ascension" instead of "accession": "We say of a king that he ascended the throne, but never speak of his *ascension* in the abstract, nor indeed of the *ascension* of any one else, except our blessed Saviour" (p. 343). Finally, "Even with all the party-prejudice of the author in favour of Mr. Fox and his politics, he has presented the public with an historical account of the reign of George III. which may stand, without being disgraced by any comparison, on the same shelf with the volumes of Smollet [*sic*]" (p. 344). A footnote adds: "We have heard this work attributed to Mr. Campbell the Poet of Hope; but we cannot say that the report, which has reached us rests on good authority. The work, however, is not unworthy of him."

This production is hardly unrelated to the pension Campbell received from the Whig government in 1805. His own final opinion of it is evident in the fact that he did not possess a copy of it in his library to show Cyrus Redding. Shortly after Campbell's death, a Tory writer for *Fraser's* reported that "few have heard of it, fewer seen it, and still fewer read it."[3]

II   Specimens of the British Poets

The prose work upon which Campbell labored longest and hardest is *Specimens of the British Poets; with Biographical and Critical Notices, and an Essay on English Poetry,* published in seven volumes in 1819. During the years of its composition, beginning in 1804 with tentative plans, he published little poetry except "Gertrude of Wyoming," but he did prepare his "Lectures on Poetry." Careful scholarship was neither his forte nor his delight, and the lack of an amanuensis made his labor all the slower and more exasperating in the checking of details.

Part of Campbell's method of procedure was to solicit the help of numerous friends, whom he considered "first-rate judges" of the individual poets, to recommend their best passages to serve as "specimens." These opinions, along with "general opinion," would determine his choices. He asked Scott to mark passages in Chatterton and also to seek the assistance of William Erskine in reading "Falconer's Shipwreck" (Beattie, 1:420–21). At the outset, he told Scott: " 'The task of this compilation appears easy; but to be well discharged, it is really fatiguing' " (*Ibid.*, p. 421).

In January 1809, after he had given up with Constable and completed arrangements with John Murray to publish the collection and to supply him with the books he needed, he wrote a long letter to his friend John Richardson setting forth his aims:

"The plan of the work is a selection of all the genuine English Poetry that can be condensed within reasonable bounds, with literary and biographical dissertations prefixed to each of the poets. I shall admit no specimen that is not of either already acknowledged excellence, or of such excellence as, if hitherto unnoticed, I may not be able to vindicate and point out. There is much excellent poetry in our language which no collector has to this day had the good sense to insert in any compilation; and there is a considerable portion which is either unknown to the bulk of more tasteful readers, or known and admired among individuals only, and never rescued from neglect by any popular notice. The men of taste seem to keep those admired passages, like mistresses, for their own insulated attachment. I wish to see them brought before the public for general admiration."

Campbell said he had full confidence in both his internal and external resources " 'to say a good deal of English Poetry, which has not yet been said,' " and added: " 'I hope to make the narrative and biographical part as accurate, as the critical and illustrative part will, I trust, be original and amusing.' "

In the short biographies he intended to keep to the main stream, leaving to antiquaries the exploration of tributaries. He would try to group the minor poets philosophically as well as "analyze them individually"—a labor that would be easier with the older poets than with the more recent ones; major writers like Milton he planned to treat in all attributes. Then, " 'Last of all, but first in the printing, will be a prefatory essay on the history and characteristics of English Poetry.' " Such an essay would be " 'a serious attempt,' " in which he would do his best. His aim was to have the whole project completed within a year, barring " 'any untoward event' " or " 'uncommon bad health' " (Beattie, 1:505–507). Ten years later, after many untoward events and various problems, Campbell did largely complete his intentions.

The opening "Essay on English Poetry" traces briefly the history of the English language, especially the influence of the Norman Conquest; discusses types and periods of literature; and introduces the poets from Chaucer through Pope. His comments on Elizabethan poetry contain an ironic foreshadowing of modern critics' problems with his own:

The fashion of the present day is to solicit public esteem not only for the best and better, but for the humblest and meanest writers of the age of Elizabeth. It is a bad book which has not something good in it; and even some

of the worst writers of that period have their twinkling beauties. . . . Men
like to make the most of the slightest beauty which they can discover in an
obsolete versifier; and they quote perhaps the solitary good thought which is
to be found in such a writer, omitting any mention of the dreary passages
which surround it. . . . When the reader however repairs to him, he finds
that there are only one or two grains of gold in all the sands of this imaginary
Pactolus. . . . It seems to be taken for granted, that the inspiration of the
good old times descended to the very lowest dregs of its versifiers.

He continues, criticizing the anthologizers:

Yet there are men who, to all appearance, would wish to revive such
authors—not for the mere use of the antiquary, to whom every volume *may*
be useful, but as standards of manner, and objects of general admiration.
Books, it is said, take up little room. In the library this may be the case; but it
is not so in the minds and time of those who peruse them. Happily indeed,
the task of pressing indifferent authors on the public attention is a fruitless
one. They may be dug up from oblivion, but life cannot be put into their
reputations. "Can these bones live?" Nature will have her course, and dull
books will be forgotten in spite of bibliographers.[4]

Campbell's moral stance comes out in his comments on James
Shirley:

Shirley was the last of our good old dramatists. When his works shall be given
to the public, they will undoubtedly enrich our popular literature. His
language sparkles with the most exquisite images. Keeping some occasional
pruriencies apart, the fault of his age rather than of himself, he speaks the
most polished and refined dialect of the stage; and even some of his
over-heightened scenes of voluptuousness are meant, though with a very
mistaken judgment, to inculcate morality. I consider his genius, indeed, as
rather brilliant and elegant than strong or lofty (p. 129).

Then Campbell the poet reveals his own predilections in judging
Shirley the poet: "From a general impression of his works I should not
paint his Muse with the haughty form and features of inspiration, but
with a countenance, in its happy moments, arch, lovely, and
interesting, both in smiles and in tears; crowned with flowers, and not
unindebted to ornament, but wearing the drapery and chaplet with a
claim to them from natural beauty" (p. 194).

In his comments on Cowley, Campbell again unintentionally
describes himself: "There is much in Cowley that will stand. He

teems, in many places, with the imagery, the feeling, the grace and gaiety of a poet. Nothing but a severer judgment was wanting to collect the scattered lights of his fancy. His unnatural flights arose less from affectation than self-deception. He cherished false thoughts as men often associate with false friends, not from insensibility to the difference between truth and falsehood, but from being too indolent to examine the difference" (p. 200).

The remarks on Pope that touched off the great Pope controversy express Campbell's differences with Pope's then recent editor, William Lisle Bowles, who, according to Campbell, "lays great stress upon the argument, that Pope's images are drawn from art more than from nature." Campbell argues:

That Pope was neither so insensible to the beauties of nature, nor so indistinct in describing them, as to forfeit the character of a genuine poet, is what I mean to urge, without exaggerating his picturesqueness. . . . I would beg leave to observe, in the first place, that the faculty by which a poet luminously describes objects of art, is essentially the same faculty, which enables him to be a faithful describer of simple nature; in the second place, that nature and art are to a greater degree relative terms in poetical description that is generally recollected; and, thirdly, that artificial objects and manners are of so much importance in fiction, as to make the exquisite description of them no less characteristic of genius, than the description of simple physical appearances.—The poet is "creation's heir." He deepens our social interest in existence (pp. 224–25).

It becomes a matter of definition:

Nature is the poet's goddess; but by nature, no one rightly understands her mere inanimate face—however charming it may be—or the simple landscape painting of trees, clouds, precipices, and flowers.—Why then try Pope, or any other poet, exclusively by his powers of describing inanimate phenomena? Nature, in the wide and proper sense of the word, means life in all its circumstances—nature moral as well as external (pp. 225–26).

After citing several examples of Pope's painting of external objects to prove that he did describe such, Campbell continues, quoting what was really Bowles's most outrageous statement:

"The true poet," says that writer, "should have an eye attentive to and familiar with every change of season, every variation of light and shade of nature, every rock, every tree, and every leaf in her secret places.—He who has not an eye to observe these, and who cannot with a glance distinguish every hue in her variety, must be so far deficient in one of the essential qualities of a poet" (pp. 229–30).

Byron liked Campbell's *Poets*, especially his "glorious" defense of Pope. That he read it carefully and marked many of Campbell's errors for correction is evident in a letter to John Murray from Ravenna on May 20, 1820:

Murray, my dear, make my respects to Thomas Campbell, and tell him from me, with faith and friendship, three things that he must right in his Poets: [Here Byron notes errors in Campbell's statements about Christopher Anstey, Cowper, and Burns (in Burns a misquotation from Shakespeare).] Now, Tom is a fine fellow; but he should be correct; for the first is an *injustice* (to Anstey), the 2nd an *ignorance,* and the third a *blunder.* Tell him all this, and let him take it in good part; for I might have rammed it into a review and vexed him—instead of which, I act like a Christian.[5]

In his diary for January 10, 1821, Byron noted that he had been marking more errors. "A good work, though—style affected—but his defense of Pope is glorious. To be sure, it is his *own cause* too, but no matter, it is very good, and does him great credit." Byron stated that he had been reading the *Lives,* but "I rarely read their works, unless an occasional flight over the classical ones, Pope, Dryden, Johnson, Gray, and those who approach them nearest."[6] On January 12, confined by bad weather and still reading the *Poets,* he commented: "There is a good deal of taffeta in some of Tom's prefatory phrases, but his work is good as a whole. I like him best, though, in his own poetry."[7]

Other critics agreed with Byron's judgments. On the more negative side was Henry Crabb Robinson, who wrote in his diary for April 9, 1820, that in reading Campbell's "Essay" he had not been "greatly edified." In his estimation, the work "contains very ordinary opinions in an unequal style; he writes prose laboriously and ambitiously, and his images do not unite originality with felicity. . . ." The next day, after reading some of the first volume of the selections, he noted: "It is not possible to make an uninteresting compilation from our older poems; but Campbell is not the man to direct the taste in such a research."[8]

More favorable in opinion was Allan Cunningham, who called the selections "in general, judicious, and such as showed the peculiar talents of the writers," and the criticisms "distinguished for taste, liberality, and acuteness."[9] Thomas Carlyle recommended the *Specimens* to his brother John for general reading, terming both the criticisms and the pieces good, with volume one a good introduction to the poets.[10]

Blackwood's welcomed the set as meeting a real need for "philosophical criticism on poetry by poets" to correct the "careless insensibility" or superciliousness of professional critics.[11] The reviewer devoted two articles to Campbell's "admirable work" (p. 708), using it in part as a springboard for his own philosophy. Among Campbell's merits that he pointed out are his ability to recognize "poetry wherever he finds it," his "pure and gentle affection towards all the productions of poetry," his "zeal for the vindication of poets from the aspersions of criticism," his "desire to redeem them from their own impurities," and the "ease and pleasure" with which the "Essay" leads along the mind of the reader" (p. 698). Also, Campbell "will not dwell on that which does not please him" (p. 699). His method of sketching "form and features" without going into full detail provides a good guide for further study. The selections are trustworthy, and the criticisms "show a singular nicety and precision of examination" (p. 700). In his simple, clear, and spirited prose style Campbell here "will surprise many of those who, having known . . . [him] only in his poetry, may have been disposed to accuse him of too elaborate and diligent contrivance of ornamented expression" (p. 702).

Francis Jeffrey, who had already lamented Campbell's small output of poetry, wrote, "We would rather see Mr Campbell as a poet, than as a commentator on poetry," but he welcomed the "very excellent and delightful" new work anyway, only wishing more of it were original.[12] He termed Campbell well qualified to judge poetry and thought he had been fair in presenting the various schools.

Again Jeffrey did not let his friendship with Campbell stand in the way of his duties as a critic, and he pointed out several flaws. The "Essay" and the biographical and critical notices "are somewhat inartificially blended,—and the latter, and most important, rather unduly anticipated and invaded, in order to enlarge the former. The only biography or criticism which we have upon Dryden, for example, is contained in the Preliminary Essay" (p. 462). On some authors Campbell has said nothing in either place; for example, he gives only the dates of Swift's life. "Sometimes the notices are entirely biographical, and sometimes entirely critical. We humbly conceive they ought always to have been of both descriptions. At all events, we think we ought in every case to have had some criticism,—since this could always have been had, and could scarcely have failed to be valuable. Mr C., we think, has been a little lazy" (p. 463). The extracts of the nearly two hundred and fifty authors are not always well selected; a few are too long, and others too short. Also,

There is a good deal of the poet's waywardness even in Mr C.'s prose. His historical Muse is as disdainful of drudgery and plain work as any of her more tuneful sisters;—and so we have things begun and abandoned—passages of great eloquence and beauty followed up by others not a little careless and disorderly—a large outline rather meagerly filled up, but with some morsels of exquisite finishing scattered irregularly up and down its expanse—little fragments of detail and controversy—and abrupt and impatient conclusions. Altogether, however, the work is very spirited; and abounds with the indications of a powerful and fine understanding, and of a delicate and original taste (p. 472).

Other reviews likewise were largely favorable. The *British Critic* found the "Essay" "too poetical" but still sound and correct, and the selections, for the present, "the best 'Corpus' of our own Poets now in existence."[13] The *Monthly Review* called Campbell's eulogies "rather capricious, and always too short," the "Essay" "masterly," and the tone of the whole "affectionate." The reviewer hoped "a kindred spirit and an equal genius" will someday perform for Campbell the office "which he has here performed for others."[14] One "Bryan Braintree," in the *Gentleman's Magazine* for April 1821, pointed out some of Campbell's errors which needed correcting[15] and Leigh Hunt, in his *Sketches of the Living Poets*, the one on Campbell dated August 21, 1821, perceived that "there is a constant struggle in him between the poetical and the critical," with much of Campbell's criticism only "ingenious and elegant writing." "In his prose he is always slipping from an exercise foreign to his nature into mere grace and fancy."[16]

Although Campbell had anticipated a revised and enlarged edition of his *Poets* to follow the first within a reasonably short time, it was 1841 before the new edition appeared. By then his interest and health both had waned to the point that Murray had to engage Peter Cunningham, son of Allan Cunningham, to make the necessary annotations and corrections. These Cunningham did very carefully, distinguishing his notes with brackets. His efforts earned the praise of the reviewers of the new edition, including George Henry Lewes in the *Westminster Review* of October 1841, the *New Monthly* for September 1841, and *Fraser's Magazine* in March 1842. The ten-page article in *Fraser's* analyzes the work, and in addition to complimenting both Campbell and Cunningham, expresses appreciation to Murray for bringing it out in an edition not only elegant but portable and extremely cheap in price.[17]

III   *Lectures on Poetry and Other Periodical Articles*

Campbell's correspondence in 1816 indicates that Murray had purchased the manuscripts of his public lectures on poetry with the intention of publishing them. At one time, the "Essay on English Poetry" and the *Specimens* were to have been a part of the much larger field that the lectures would cover when completed. (In the lectures, Campbell's ambition was to survey the entire history of world literature, including the modern European literatures. In preparation, he studied the original languages, but the project was too vast for him to accomplish.) He engaged in correspondence with Murray about the timing of the two publications and the possible effects of one being published first. What finally happened with Murray beyond publication of the *Specimens* is not clear, but Campbell never brought out the lectures in book form as he had intended.

When he became editor of the *New Monthly*, he rewrote them and published them over a period of time from January 1821 until November 1826 as "Lectures on Poetry, the Substance of Which Was Delivered at the Royal Institution." He confused his numbering, so that he omitted numbers eight and nine, called the first half of seven number nine, and called ten lectures twelve. In Lecture I he discussed poetical composition; in II, Hebrew Poetry; and from III on, Greek Poetry, getting through Euripides.

For his efforts, Campbell received a number of favorable comments. "Christopher North" [John Wilson] liked them.[18] So did Hazlitt, who remarked in "The Spirit of the Age" that "Mr. Campbell's prose-criticisms on contemporary and other poets (which have appeared in the New Monthly Magazine) are in a style at once chaste, temperate, guarded, and just."[19] Cyrus Redding, Campbell's subeditor on the *New Monthly*, stated in his *Literary Reminiscences:* "There is nothing in prose which Campbell did, either in regard to writing, analysis, or a philosophical view of any subject he ever

treated, better than his opening lecture. It is, in all points, masterly."[20] A recent writer, discussing Campbell's influence on Emerson, called Lecture I "probably . . . Campbell's best critical effort"
and an "important critique of Bacon's view of poetry" which helped
shape Emerson's development of poetic theory. (Emerson read the
Philadelphia reprint of the *New Monthly*.)[21]

On the negative side, a writer who signed himself "D." addressed a
letter to the editor of *Blackwood's* accusing Campbell "of not
acknowledging, 1st, That he is indebted to Frederic Schlegel for
numerous conclusions, which must have been the result of long and
arduous study; and 2d, That he has transplanted into his lectures,
(particularly the *third*, fourth, and fifth,) whole rows of classical
references, which Schlegel originally collected and methodized."
Citing examples to show that Campbell used Schlegel's "very rare"
work rather than the original Homer, he holds that Campbell should
confess his obligations, especially since he "has just commenced a
series of Letters, (on Greek Literature,) addressed to the students at
Glasgow College."[22]

These "Letters to the Students of Glasgow" ran in the *New
Monthly* from July 1827 until August 1828. Campbell's purpose was
to give a general introduction to "the chief epochs of literature" in
order to interest the students in further study. This time he began
with the Greeks and got up to the Romans, including a great deal of
history in his survey.

For the periodicals Campbell wrote other articles on poetry, such
as a review of Percival Stockdale's *Lectures on the truly Eminent
English Poets* (1807) for the *Edinburgh Review* in April 1808, when he
was starting his own *Specimens*. Of the twenty-one pages, Pope
occupies five. Like other reviewers, Campbell argued with the
author and incorporated his own ideas into his essay.

IV Life of Mrs. Siddons

Despite his idolization of Mrs. Siddons, Campbell wrote a very
faulty biography of her. From his young manhood on he had looked
upon her as more than a great actress: she was the embodiment of the
noble woman. His adulation was such that Cyrus Redding, who also
knew her, enjoyed playing the iconoclast. To Redding she was indeed
a great tragic actress, but a very ordinary woman. He records telling
Campbell: "She was majestic, certainly, but not very feminine. You

are a little man, and little men, they say, are fond of giantesses, and gigantic men of little women."[23]

Burdened by his emotions, his health, and other commitments at the time, Campbell found the writing of Mrs. Siddons' life a difficult undertaking. His sensitivity about his recent failure on Lawrence's biography did not help. Redding, who was associated with Campbell at the time he was working on it, deemed him unsuited for the task. Besides, said Redding, "There can be no record of mind in the saying of those whose lives are spent in doing no more than repeating the sayings of others, the whole matter being as to whether those sayings are well or ill declaimed."[24] Redding had still more to say on the subject: "The incidents in the life of an actress of the highest class, of staid manners, and plain good sense, could not be expected to abound in incident." Her life was too "lofty in feeling and pure in morals" to make an interesting biography. "Though the greatest actress that ever trod the stage, her real excellencies could not be described, more than half of them depending upon vision." Aside from her acting, "She was not a woman of genius; and she was not a woman of reading beyond her profession. The poet owned himself that a young girl would write letters as good as those of Mrs. Siddons. . . . Nor in her conversation . . . was there anything worthy of record upon paper." Further, Campbell was only a spectator at the theater, not one who mingled with the actors and knew "the *patois* of the theatre." His temperament "had no affinity with the artificial theatre-going folk."[25]

Nevertheless, bound by his promise to her, Campbell set about collecting all the materials he could find about Mrs. Siddons in addition to those memoirs she had left him. He wrote and visited members of her family and talked with persons who had known her and her family. Much of what he obtained was useless, and he kept searching for additional materials about the theater to supplement the personal items.

After he had written two chapters, he discussed with John Payne Collier the temptation of a joint authorship. Difficulties in such a project included responsibility, style (especially regarding personal recollections), possible differences in appreciation of Mrs. Siddons' character, and recognition on the title page for Collier's share in the work. Finally, Campbell's compunctions of conscience about his obligation combined with these problems, plus Collier's evident unwillingness to work without due recognition, to end any ideas of co-authorship. Campbell was very anxious not to appear to be abandoning the undertaking, and he positively did not want any advance advertising of a joint authorship about which his friends would rally him. He was concerned about producing a substantial work that would sell well, even with the 1827 *Memoirs of Mrs. Siddons* by James Boaden already on the market.[26]

During the period of their discussions, Collier had corresponded with Mrs. Ann Julia Kemble Hatton, seeking memoirs of her famous sister. Mrs. Hatton, old, ill, poverty-stricken, and resentful that Mrs. Siddons had not done better by her in her will, offered to bargain with him—to supply memoirs in return for assistance in publishing a little collection of her poems. After a short time, she did supply ten pages of memoirs, now in the Folger Library, which Campbell could use in his work.

The *Life of Mrs. Siddons* begins with Campbell's memories of her parents and anecdotes about her famous family. In twenty chapters totaling two hundred sixty pages, it moves through her acting career and death to a "General Eulogium on her Character." Chapter III is a history of "Females on the English Stage," giving the "Names and Characters of Mrs. Siddons's greatest Predecessors." In the "Eulogium," Campbell states his own appreciation:

In speaking of her as an actress, my predominant sensation, while writing her Life, has been a consciousness of my incompetence to do her justice. Her lofty beauty, her graceful walk and gesture, and her potent elocution, were endowments which at the first sight marked her supremacy on the stage. . . . But it was the high judgment which watched over all these qualifications, the equally vigilant sympathy which threw itself into the assumed character,—it was her sustained understanding of her part, her self-devotion to it, and her abstraction from every thing else, and no casual bursts of effect, that riveted the experienced spectator's admiration.

He goes on to pay tribute to her personal character, emphasizing "the benignity of her disposition." In manner she was grave, with "no powers for brilliancy in mixed conversation." She was "a great, simple being, who was not shrewd in her knowledge of the world, and was not herself well understood in some particulars by the majority of the world." Feeling that his "heart regrets and honours her with all its sincerity," he concludes that "she was more than a woman of genius; for the additional benevolence of her heart made her an honour to her sex and to human nature."[27]

Redding terms the work "a biography on stilts," written in a style "foreign to that of his former works." When Campbell "thought he was earnest and effective, he was really inflated and unprofitable. Yet the book is not worthless. "If he has not produced anything that has conferred additional fame upon his literary character, still he has said all that could be said, and left unrecorded nothing that such a subject would admit of being recorded in its regard, but he has erred, and egregiously too, in the manner of saying it."[28]

Among the numerous notices the work received, the most derogatory was the *Quarterly Review*'s, written by John Wilson Croker.[29] "The book," he began, is "a real *superfetation*," "worse than unnecessary" with Boaden's production already available. It is a "work of supererogation" and an "*abuse of biography*" that "can add nothing to the reputation of either the object or the author." The only new things in it are "a few pages of autobiographical memoranda, a couple of prosy dissertations on the characters of Constance and Lady Macbeth, and three or four very unimportant letters" (p. 95). Because of its "obscure bombast," Croker is inclined to believe a rumor that Campbell "ought rather to be considered as the editor than as the substantial author of this book" (p. 96). To corroborate his charges, he cites numerous examples of poor style, inept word choice, irreverent tone, digressions, inaccuracies in fact, and other sources quoted incorrectly or without acknowledgement. Such "inconsistency and negligence" surely indicate a lack of editorial correction. Worked up to hyperbole, Croker complains that "there is nothing original but his blunders" (p. 110). "Undoubtedly the best pages in the book," Mrs. Siddons' "autobiographical memoranda," are too short, and Campbell does not handle them satisfactorily. Were they "a continuous narrative, out of which he has only selected a few passages"? (p. 113). Another fault is Campbell's failure to provide contemporary evidence of Mrs. Siddons' early career. Although she was "*the greatest tragic actress that ever lived*" (p. 123), Campbell is "the worst theatrical historian we have ever read." He is "a distinguished poet" and "a man of undoubted genius," but he has strayed out of his field (p. 124).

Other reviews, some of them citing long passages from the work, were less virulent. A few, like the *Athenaeum*'s, noted the difficulty Campbell had in working with his materials to turn them into "a very creditable biography."[30] The *Gentleman's Magazine* wished he had published more of her private correspondence to show "Mrs. Siddons herself" instead of displaying largely her public character, which Boaden had already done.[31] *Tait's Edinburgh Magazine* thought the most valuable part of the work was "Mr. Campbell's observations on dramatic poetry, and on particular plays."[32] That reviewer wished he had not "fancied himself bound, in biographic decorum, or social propriety, to suppress . . . the many characteristic traits and anecdotes with which he has the power of interweaving a *Boswellian* life of the great actress, if he might shew the will" (p. 479).

The *Monthly Review* complimented Campbell for losing sight of himself "in order to preserve the simplicity of his narrative. Still, there is no want of that fine spirit, that forcible style, that grace and polish for which Mr. Campbell is so justly celebrated."[33] It goes further: "We admire greatly Mrs. Siddon's [*sic*] career, as the colleague, so to speak, of Shakespeare, and look upon the history of her love for him, and perfected union, to be better and more interesting than most romantic attachments. But what would this union have seemed, if treated by coarser hands than those of the author of Gertrude of Wyoming?" (p. 440). The *Literary Gazette* similarly judged that "it is a happy chance to have so gifted a friend to preserve . . . for a time to come" Mrs. Siddons' "life and splendid dramatic triumphs."[34]

The strongest antidote to Croker's criticism appeared in the *New Monthly Magazine* at about the same time as his Tory condemnation came out in the *Quarterly*.[35] That unknown reviewer's eulogy said in part: "Mr. Campbell has forcibly revived the public impression of his great talents, in conveying what is erudite and profound, in a manner clear, chaste and warm even to fascination" (p. 470). With hyperbole matching Croker's, it continues: "He elicits new beauties, elucidates by illustration, impresses by kindred feeling, and illuminates by that clear, brilliant and captivating character of genius, which is so conspicuous in all his writings, and in which the individual shines irresistibly through the author" (p. 474). The work is even "calculated to raise our moral character by the freshness and cheerful vigour, with the healthy analysis of our passions and actions, which, to the author's honour, shine in every chapter. There are many beautiful sentiments and fine discriminations, which may cleanse present society of the cant and morbid confusion with which it is so disordered" (p. 474).

So went the war with words.

V   Letters from the South

Leaving the tumult behind him, Campbell took off for the Continent within a week after the biography was published. From there his capricious behavior, touched off partly by a previous interest in Africa, turned him toward Algeria.

In December 1830, he had published an article in the *New Monthly* on "Thoughts and Facts Respecting the Civilization of Africa," occasioned by the French conquest of that country in 1830.[36] In that essay he advocated that Britain "cope with France for the confidence of Egypt," not through war but "with pacific vigilance," applying "British sagacity and enterprise" to the regeneration of Egypt (which had already begun), to make Egypt "a vast field for human happiness and improvement, and . . . an accession to the wealth of the whole habitable globe" (p. 520). What he had in mind was not conquest and colonization, but a new idea: "enlightening those barbarous people through and with their own leaders, in guiding their measures by a prudent exertion of influence, and by carrying sound principles of international law *actively*, but not dictatorially, into their councils" (p. 526). Britain and France could cooperate to abolish "the overland slave trade of Africa," a "horrible traffic" (p. 527), and aid in the civilization of African blacks, who are certainly capable of improvement; witness "the Griquas, in Southern Africa," Sierra Leone, Liberia, and Haiti (p. 529).

Now, to see for himself the effects of the French conquest on African civilization was his avowed objective. In his preface to the collected *Letters*, he says he was the first Englishman to visit Algiers for that purpose. Although he had hoped the French were "opening . . . the northern gate of civilization into Africa; and preparing the way for commerce and intelligence, to expand over a large space of the globe," the "gross errors" he had found them making disappointed him. At the present there was some question about whether the French would even retain the colony.[37]

In its book form *Letters from the South*, published by Henry Colburn in 1837, reprints in two volumes the twenty-five letters previously printed in the *New Monthly* with an added appendix on Algeria. In episodic arrangement, it not only recounts Campbell's travels, but provides a lively geography of Algeria in all of its aspects, replete with an assortment of entertaining anecdotes, news, and commentary of human interest. An example of a letter in the *New Monthly* is his description of the Moorish women:

The streets of Algiers, as I have told you, are very dismal; and really, when you meet a Moorish woman, under their gloom, in a drapery much resembling the dress of our dead in England, and looking as much as possible like a mummy or a ghost, she is far from inspiring gallant sensations. Where you have light to see them, the bandiness of their legs is generally observable under their shrouds, and the shrivelled skin around their eyes indicates that there is no great cruelty in their veiling themselves. Still I must own that I have not seen the Moorish ladies so as to judge of them fairly.[38]

The reviews noticed the entertainment value of the work. *Tait's Edinburgh Magazine* observed that

the letters themselves are lively, playful, waggish, hilarious, and redolent of the jocund spirit of youth, with just as much serious feeling as a poet who is a man of the world, cares to exhibit. They may not contain a very remarkable quantity of *useful knowledge.* So much the better. . . . The charm of his letters is personal narrative . . . told with a sprightly and charming facil- ity. . . . The poet breaks out in many of his descriptions; and his images are often those of the finest poetry.[39]

Other reviews, including the *Monthly* and the *Athenaeum,* found the *Letters* gossipy and amusing enough to extract long specimens for their readers, but not a work for critics to analyze. The *Eclectic Review* also recommended the publication as entertainment, but wished Campbell would bestir himself from his indolence and fitfulness and use his talents to write more poetry like "The Pleasures of Hope," instead of prose, which is only his avocation and amuse- ment.[40]

VI   The Scenic Annual

Campbell surprised his friends by permitting his name to be used as editor of *The Scenic Annual, for 1838.* The reviewers who noticed the work briefly were also surprised, but judged that his celebrated name should give the work success. The *New Monthly* writers described the gift book: "The volume is a quarto, as showily bound as the crowd of those engravings deriving additional value from illus- trations in both prose and verse, some by the hand of the poet himself, and the rest chosen with his approbation. The scenery consists chiefly of foreign views, but there are some of marked beauty, selected from the landscape of Scotland; the whole forming a very splendid performance." They were happy to see some new poetry by Campbell and appreciated his "neat and playful preface."[41]

The *Gentleman's Magazine* complimented the "selection of scen- ery," the "skill and elegance of composition," and the "pleasing and picturesque effect in the engravings" of the volume, which far surpasses its rivals "in the splendour of the editor's reputation." After quoting three of Campbell's poems from the volume, "Cora Linn," "Lines suggested by a Picture of the Statue of Arnold Von Winkelried," and "Chaucer," the reviewer concluded with verses about Campbell himself:

> So in spite of his years,
> And his trip to Algiers,
> Mr. Campbell again
> Has his poetic vein;
> And we hope, though the subject's unpleasant to mention,
> That his poetry now will secure him—his Pension.[42]

Whether any enlargement of his pension was in the back of his mind or not, Campbell, upon hearing that the Queen had borrowed the book and "had been highly delighted with it," ordered copies of his poems and *Letters from the South* to be "royally bound" for presentation to Her Majesty. Before her officer in charge of such matters would consent to receive them, however, Campbell had to assure him that the Queen would be incurring no obligation to accept his token of loyalty to her, that he was not coveting any advantage in desiring her to read his works. Victoria did accept the volumes and requested that Campbell autograph them. Later he attended her first levee and was presented to her by the Duke of Argyll.

VII   The Dramatic Works of Shakspeare

Campbell's edition of *The Dramatic Works of Shakspeare, with remarks on his life and writings*, appeared in two editions during his lifetime, in 1838 and 1843, followed by others in 1848, 1863, and 1866. It is a popular, not a scholarly, edition of Shakespeare. Although Redding terms Campbell's part "utterly worthless"[43] and the reviewers largely ignored the volume, a recent *History of Shakespearian Criticism* is kinder:

Campbell makes no great discoveries, but his criticism has a certain freshness. He records his experience of Shakespeare truly, uninfluenced by the immense amount of commentary which has preceded him. Often it is little more than a mere statement of personal preferences—e.g. his words on Julia and Beatrice and on *Timon*. And he can condone the improbabilities of *Cymbeline* because the story pleased him, but not those of *M. for M.* But on the whole he is saved from serious lapses by his genuine poetic feeling. He is a poet, though a small one, and as such he can touch the hem of Shakespeare's garment—though no more. His most successful remarks are on *All's Well*, *A. Y. L.*, and *Twelfth-Night*. His nearest fellow-critic is the German Heine.[44]

In his comments on Shakespeare, whom he genuinely admired, Campbell again reveals himself. For instance, in discussing the woman of the sonnets, he remarks,

I have a suspicion . . . that if the love affair had been real, he would have said less about it. Nevertheless I am far from entertaining the opinion that Shakspeare never felt the passion of love for any other woman than his wife Anne Hathaway. She married him, or rather perhaps decoyed him into a marriage, when she was in her twenty-sixth year, and when he was a boy of eighteen. Setting aside the suspicion of Susanna Shakspeare's birth having been premature for her mother's reputation, the very circumstance of a full grown woman marrying a stripling of eighteen, is discreditable to her memory, and leaves us with no great sympathy for her, if Shakspeare, amidst the allurements of London, forgot his conjugal faith.[45]

He speaks with wonder of Shakespeare's "seeming unconcern, either about his own fame, or about the interest which the world was to take in him" (pp. ix-x). Then, in a footnote, he speculates on the major reasons for the loss of Shakespeare's manuscripts: "the accident of fire" and "the sloth of his contemporaries." The burning of the Globe theater, of much of the town of Stratford, of Ben Jonson's house and library, and of a great part of London in 1666 account for at least some of the losses (p. x).

Campbell shows that he has read the work of the Shakespearean scholars up to his time by commenting on and differing with their hypotheses, both on Shakespeare's life and theatrical background and on the plays. He ends his remarks on *Much Ado About Nothing* with a personal judgment:

Mrs. Jameson, in her characters of Shakspeare's women, concludes with hoping that Beatrice will live happy with Benedick; but I have no such hope; and my final anticipation in reading the play is the certainty that Beatrice will provoke her Benedick to give her much and just conjugal castigation. She is an odious woman. . . .

I once knew such a pair: the lady was a perfect Beatrice; she railed hypocritically at wedlock before her marriage, and with bitter sincerity after it. She and her Benedick now live apart, but with entire reciprocity of sentiments, each devoutly wishing that the other may soon pass into a better world. Beatrice is not to be compared, but contrasted with Rosalind, who is equally witty: but the sparkling sayings of Rosalind are like gems upon her head at court, and like dew-drops on her bright hair in the woodland forest. (p. xlvi)

In this rather hastily done project, Campbell's old age shows, and it is not an accomplishment in which he could take much pride.

VIII   Life of Petrarch

Neither did his *Life of Petrarch* (1841) add to his reputation or provide any new information about the great Italian writer. It is to Campbell's credit, however, that he abandoned his original project of merely editing Archdeacon Coxe's verbose and incomplete manuscript for a fee of two hundred pounds and tried instead to produce something better. What he did not realize was that his own lack of time, scholarly patience, and wide background in Italian literature and history were limitations to his ability to produce a significant biography.

As he states in the "Advertisement" preceding the preface to his book, he largely followed the standard text of the Abbé de Sade, correcting it "by the aid of . . . [Petrarch's] latest biographer Baldelli." In his preface, he surveys the history of Petrarchan biography, with an evaluation of each writer. Then the two-volume life begins with a statement on Petrarch's importance to literature, traces his full and busy life and loves against the political and religious background of his age, and ends with a "Summary of Petrarch's character, moral, political, and poetical." Petrarch, says Campbell, was

a restorer of ancient learning, a rescuer of its treasures from oblivion, a despiser of many contemporary superstitions, a man, who, though no reformer himself, certainly contributed to the reformation, . . . an Italian patriot who was above provincial partialities, a poet who still lives in the hearts of his country, and who is shielded from oblivion by more generations than there were hides in the seven-fold shield of Ajax—if this was not a great man, many who are so called must bear the title unworthily. He was a faithful friend, and a devoted lover, and appears to have been one of the most fascinating beings that ever existed.[46]

The *Gentleman's Magazine*, noting Campbell's "genuine sympathy with Petrarch," welcomed the book, "the history of a poet, written by one of kindred feeling and inspiration."[47] Later, when the *Life* was reprinted in an English translation of Petrarch's poetry, that magazine called Campbell's "admirable general criticism on the poetry" a good introduction to the translations themselves.[48]

The *Athenaeum* devoted a two-part notice to the work, observing that Campbell,

both as author and as man, . . . is so simple, so natural, and so unaffected, that the character of his work might have been foretold on the simple announcement of its title. There could be little hesitation in pre-determining that his Life of Petrarch would be a reflection of his own image of the man, unsophisticated by pedantic alembication, unstained by preconceived theories, but refined perhaps and exalted by the tint of his own views of human nature, and his own poetic temperament.[49]

As for the question of Laura's existence and the nature of Petrarch's passion for her, "we are presented with the common-sense side of the question, the side now most universally received." Campbell "writes almost wholly under the influence of his affections. He seems ever in search of traces of human nature, and evidently more delights in the portraiture of the man, than of the poet. There is even a shade of Scotch homeliness in his mode of treating his theme" (p. 379). The reviewer concluded that he was glad "to bear testimony to the vigorous health of his [Campbell's] literary climacteric" (p. 402).

Tait's Edinburgh Magazine thought it "by far the best book which has yet appeared" on Petrarch, even though in producing it Campbell "may not . . . have added much to his high literary reputation."[50] Much of it is written "in the happiest vein of slip-shod; but with justness and often felicity of thought, easy mother-wit, and, above all, genial good-nature, and marked superiority to cant and pedantry." It has "as much genuine learning, without its repulsive seeming, as the reading public are disposed to tolerate in a popular work," for now lives of poets are written "for the men and women of the working-day world" (p. 529). Two passages from the book that the critic quotes show not only Campbell's "common sense" but also Campbell's attitudes: "Of the two persons in this love affair, I am more inclined to pity Laura than Petrarch. Independently of her personal charms, I cannot conceive Laura otherwise than as a kind-hearted, loveable woman, who could not well be supposed to be totally indifferent to the devotion of the most famous and fascinating man of his age" (p.

531). Again, "it is said that Petrarch, if it had not been for this passion, would not have been the poet that he was. Not, perhaps, so good an amatory poet; but I firmly believe that he would have been a more various and masculine, and, upon the whole, *a greater poet*, if he had never been bewitched by Laura" (p. 532). As to Petrarch's other love: "With all his philosophy and platonic raptures about Laura, Petrarch was still subject to the passions of ordinary men, and had a mistress at Avignon who was kinder to him than Laura" (p. 532). Campbell thought Petrarch heartless to have consigned this mistress' name to oblivion after she sacrificed her reputation for him.

The *Spectator* was severe with Campbell's "elegant but feeble tenuity, and a kind of grave twaddling, in which thoughts not unjust in themselves are marred by their style. . . . Neither do some occasional efforts at facetiousness relieve the tame character of the composition, though they no doubt somewhat diversify its level." Worse than defects of style, however, is Campbell's lack of any "original knowledge of Petrarch or his times, and not much of reading connected with them," thereby depriving the biography of a "lifelike air." "The work upon the whole is readable, and animated by a genial spirit of *bonhommie;* but it was not *wanted.*"[51]

Another unfavorable review of Campbell's *Petrarch* appeared in *Graham's Magazine*, published in Philadelphia. According to James B. Reece, Edgar Allan Poe was the critic. To Poe the book on the whole "is unworthy Thomas Campbell—still less is it worthy Petrarch."[52] Reece suggests that, in writing his review, Poe read Campbell's accounts of the effects of the plague in Italy during Petrarch's day and that from them he quite possibly acquired the basic material for the plot of "The Masque of the Red Death."[53]

IX Frederick the Great

The real author of *Frederick the Great, His Court and Times* (1842–43), was Frederick Shoberl, but he chose anonymity. The title page says the work was "Edited, with an Introduction, by Thomas Campbell, Esq., author of 'The Pleasures of Hope,' 'The Life of Petrarch,' &c." All Campbell actually did was to write an introduction of thirteen pages, stating his consent to recommend the volumes as their "sponsor." Presenting to interested readers the Prussian monarch's accomplishments (despite his regrettable participation in the partition of Poland), he concluded with a compliment to the

Prussian people, whom he had known from his travels in their country.

X   History of Our Own Times

If the above work required little of Campbell's time and effort, one that must have required still less, if any at all, was the *History of Our Own Times*, by the author of "The Court and Times of Frederick the Great [i.e. T. Campbell]," as the British Museum Catalogue lists the two volumes published in 1843 and 1845. Shoberl was again the author, and Campbell may have written the preface.

All of his life, Campbell manufactured or lent his name to whatever the booksellers thought would sell. Never was he able to manage his pension, his legacies, and the royalties from his poems so that he could be free from the "scribbling" he so frequently complained about. In his later years, writing for the publishers helped to fill his lonely hours and to provide a good rationalization for his failure to produce more original poetry. For him, the making of money became more of a temptation than a financial necessity. In a manuscript letter now in the London University Library, he likened the offers of the publisher Henry Colburn to Atalanta's golden apples. And like Atalanta, he succumbed.

CHAPTER 7

"The 'Name Unknown' ": Campbell Today

CAMPBELL himself now is almost a "Name Unknown." His sun has set, leaving still a "shadowy tint" that, viewed from today's distance, lends little "enchantment." Yet as a minor classic poet and humanitarian with a large audience in his day, both at home and abroad, he holds a place in the great tradition of humanism in which each new generation defines its values and determines its quality of life. Through his widely quoted poems and his educational and philanthropic endeavors, he helped to free the hearts and minds of his era; therefore, to humanists of our time he offers the values of active hope.

Few poets have become famous so early or profited so much from early success as did Campbell. Many commentators have noted his good fortune in timing the appearance of "The Pleasures of Hope" in 1799 both to reflect and to help set the mood of his readers. True to his eighteenth-century heritage, he spoke as a social voice rather than as a private one, and his lyricism conflicted with his didacticism. Yet many of the ideas he expressed were romantic, and he aided the triumph of the romantic movement. The dynamism of individual yearning and striving at whatever the cost to achieve the heroic ideals that are the glory of the human race—this is the romantic quest theme of many of Campbell's poems and the same one which motivated the founders of the United States. Additional romantic characteristics of Campbell include his rebellion against tyranny, sympathy with exiles, love of the wild in nature, interest in the past, concern for the common man, and delight in children. The tension between his powerful feelings and the classical restraint and polish he thought necessary for their expression was Campbell's major problem in his poetry. Few of his poems seem genuinely spontaneous.

Other tensions imperfectly resolved plagued Campbell throughout his life: creative poetry versus prose editorial work, ambition

143

versus fulfillment, desire versus discipline, fame versus fear of its loss, and Scotland versus England. Scotland, from which he uprooted himself, signified family, friends, early training, stress on industry, and the Presbyterianism he rejected; England represented metropolitanism, gradual loss of individuality in the masses of London, financial success, indolence, and feelings of suppressed guilt. A lack of self-confidence in his writing is evident in his constant submission of his poems to his friends for critical comment.

These internal struggles contributed to the conflicting judgments of him by others. Even now, appraisals of him vary widely. In his day, when the criticism of literature often turned on political affiliations, Campbell's strong Whig partisanship frequently provoked greater censure than the actual faults of his work deserved or else higher praise than its merits were due. Contributing to the varying opinions was Campbell's position as a transitional figure in a time of changing poetic tastes. His efforts to maintain his social voice instead of freeing himself from restraint caused Scott, according to Washington Irving, to say of him: " 'What a pity it is . . . that Campbell does not write more and oftener, and give full sweep to his genius. He has wings that would bear him to the skies; and he does now and then spread them grandly, but folds them up again and resumes his perch, as if he was afraid to launch away. He don't know or won't trust his own strength.' " Another of his conflicts is that " 'Campbell is, in a manner, a bugbear to himself. The brightness of his early success is a detriment to all his further efforts. *He is afraid of the shadow that his own fame casts before him.*' "[1]

Unfortunately, Campbell's friends and literary critics expected more of him than his talent, health, self-discipline, or time permitted him to accomplish. Because of their disappointed hopes, they were sharper than they might otherwise have been in their judgments. He was more unlucky than most authors in having *soi-disant* friends who sought to line their pockets by publishing in the periodicals posthumous remembrances of him depicting his weaknesses in his declining years. Many of these articles have colored later opinions.

Although Campbell outlived his contemporaries Crabbe, Scott, Lamb, Blake, Coleridge, Byron, Shelley, and Keats, the effectiveness of his own life began diminishing rapidly with the onset of the insidious tertiary stage of his disease, producing those symptoms of premature decay and personality change noted by his acquaintances from 1825 on. He labored as well as he could, writing poetry when his health and spirits permitted. In his relegation of poetry to second place in his life's work, his health was certainly a factor.

The poems he did publish vary greatly in merit, and an individual poem may be unequal within itself. Attributes of his poetry include good taste, elegance, perspicuity, vivid imagery, good metaphors, occasionally excellent choice of language, variations of verse forms, and experiments with a new music. His best lyrics are marked by energy, simplicity, and beauty. On the other side, faults too often found are lack of clarity in narration, weaknesses in point of view and structure, inversions, overuse of apostrophe, excessive use of poetic diction, platitudes, and high-flown rhetoric. Often he loses the effectiveness of immediacy by writing in the past tense for remembered time.

Campbell's poetry is based on thought as well as feeling, for he spoke to the thinking, concerned people of his day; however, the thought is often only the obvious, conveyed with appropriate sound effects. In playing the role of poet as prophet, he could criticize his own country for what he considered its failures to place human values above diplomatic maneuvers and economic gain. Yet he had strong pride in his nationality. Thus, in the highest sense, he was a patriot who tried to make not only his country but the world a better place to live. Sincerity is the characteristic tone of his work.

In his poetry, he treated archetypal themes and characters that have inspired literature for ages of humankind: search, transformation, prophecy and fulfillment; the hero, the wise old man, the fatal woman, the earth-mother. The human drama of his day and the actors therein were his subjects, as were the myths and legends of his forebears. Despite his objective point of view, there is also more of Campbell himself in his poetry than some of his critics have noticed.

His importance as a citizen is evidenced in the position London University holds in higher education today as well as in the lasting appreciation of the Poles and the many other victims of society who benefited from his words and from his purse. Even in the pursuit of his own volitions, he was always a member of society, seldom a lone singer.

Campbell is a link in the chain of English poetry, with bonds to his predecessors and connections with his successors. Other poets whose letters or works admit Campbell's influence at least in their youth include Crabbe, Byron, Shelley, Tennyson, Browning, Elizabeth Barrett Browning, Peacock, Hopkins, Swinburne, Carlyle (who tried some early verse), Emerson, and Whittier. Arnold, in his essay "On the Study of Celtic Literature," paid tribute to his style; and Goethe, in a letter appended by Beattie, spoke of his classicism and the "strength," "great natural simplicity of style," and "power of exciting high emotions" of his poetry (2:516–17). Coleridge, who did not think Campbell would survive much beyond his day, was himself one of the giants who overshadowed Campbell, even before he (Coleridge) died in 1834.

Aside from his appreciation of good prose and his practice of it in *Specimens of the British Poets*, Campbell is remembered today for his poetry of freedom, patriotism, and human worth. Many of his lines have become proverbial quotations. Most often anthologized, along with passages from "The Pleasures of Hope," are his songs of battle, notably "Hohenlinden," "Battle of the Baltic," "Ye Mariners of England," and sometimes "The Death-Boat of Heligoland." Depending on his taste and space limitations, an editor may include some of the historical and legendary poems such as "Lochiel's Warning" and "Lord Ullin's Daughter." "The Last Man" is the miscellaneous poem easiest to find today.

Flaws are all too evident in Campbell's poems, most of which now seem old-fashioned "period pieces"; yet even the faults themselves can have historical value in revealing the past channels of English poetry and the changing responses of readers and critics. Since Campbell's day, definitions of poetry, patriotism, and freedom all have altered. As he himself said, "Nature will have her course," and versifiers do become obsolete. Nowadays those readers whose tastes respond only to the modern will relegate Campbell to the rare book shelves, but other students who appreciate their literary heritage will find their reading of a genuine poet popular at the turn of the nineteenth century rewarding, especially those poems in which Campbell treats well the universal themes of human experience.

Notes and References

Chapter One

1. William Beattie, ed., *Life and Letters of Thomas Campbell* (New York, 1850), 1: 45. Further references will be given in the text, with Beattie's quotations of Campbell's words shown in double sets of quotation marks. Note that the edition used for this study is an American reprint in two volumes.

2. Lines 17-18 read: " 'Thou shalt live,' she replied; 'Heaven's mercy relieving / Each anguishing wound, shall forbid me to mourn!' " "Fair Adelaide," thus addressing her wounded Henry, expresses confidence that speedy relief from Heaven would soon heal his wounds; the printer's error in placing a semicolon after "relieving" distorts the meaning and Adelaide's feeling.

3. Henry E. Huntington Library manuscript HM 31482, June 1, 1800. This item is reproduced by permission of the Huntington Library, San Marino, California. Beattie in 1:233–34 prints the same letter with considerable editing—omissions, word substitutes, and punctuation.

4. A fag in British usage is a menial or drudge.

5. Bodleian Library MS. Eng. Misc. d. 184.

6. Leigh Hunt, *Autobiography,* ed. Roger Ingpen (London, 1903), 1:202.

7. John Gibson Lockhart, *The Life of Sir Walter Scott* (Edinburgh, 1902–1903), 3: 341.

8. [William Hazlitt], "The Periodical Press," *Edinburgh Review,* 38 (May 1823), 371. Campbell also had his differences with Hazlitt.

9. A manuscript letter in the National Library of Scotland dated October 19, 1824, identifies Joanna Baillie as one person to whom Campbell sent proofs of the poem while it was being printed, thereby deliberately delaying the publication date.

10. "Country News," *Illustrated London News,* 5 (September 28, 1844), 195.

11. "Amicus," "Literary and Familiar Reminiscences of Thomas Campbell, Esq.," *New Monthly Magazine,* 74 (August 1845), 566.

12. "Thomas Campbell," review of *Life and Letters of Thomas Campbell, Literary Gazette,* no. 1665 (December 16, 1848), p. 817.

13. J. Logie Robertson, ed., *The Complete Poetical Works of Thomas Campbell,* Oxford ed. (London, 1907). Unless otherwise noted, all further citations of the poems are from this edition and are given in the text.

14. "Thomas Campbell," p. 818.

Chapter Two

1. *Analytical Review*, N.S. 1 (June 1799), 622–23.

2. "Campbell's Pleasures of Hope," *British Critic*, 14 (July 1799), 21–26. This quotation is from p. 21.

3. Cyrus Redding, *Literary Reminiscences and Memoirs of Thomas Campbell* (London, 1860), 1:41–42.

4. [Alexander Hamilton], "Campbell's *Pleasures of Hope*," *Monthly Review*, 29 (August 1799), 422–26. These quotations are from p. 422.

5. Alexander Dyce, ed., *Recollections of the Table-Talk of Samuel Rogers* (1856; rpt. London, 1952, ed. Morchard Bishop), p. 208.

6. Derek Hudson, ed., *The Diary of Henry Crabb Robinson* (London, 1967), pp. 22–23.

7. Richard W. Armour and Raymond F. Howes, eds., *Coleridge the Talker* (Ithaca, N.Y., 1940), pp. 175–76. Coleridge's statement about Campbell's borrowed line is at odds with the theory of Robert S. Forsythe that Campbell borrowed the line from Coleridge himself ("Freedom's Shriek," *Notes and Queries*, 150 [January 9, 1926], 23–24). Coleridge's sonnet on Kosciusko, first published in the *Morning Chronicle* in 1794 and reprinted in his *Poems on Various Subjects* in 1796, begins: "O what a loud and fearful shriek was there." Forsythe concludes that from similarities between the poems, Campbell knew Coleridge's sonnet prior to composing "The Pleasures of Hope," but Coleridge himself does not accuse Campbell of borrowing from him. Did both use a common source?

8. Lord John Russell, ed., *Memoirs, Journal, and Correspondence of Thomas Moore* (London, 1853–56), 4:335.

9. Byron, "English Bards and Scotch Reviewers," *ll. 801–802*.

10. P. P. Howe, ed., *The Complete Works of William Hazlitt* (New York, 1967), 5:149–50. Beattie (1:223) notes similar descriptions of angels' visits in Burns and Norris. Again Campbell was making use of common poetic stock.

11. Ibid., 9:243.

12. Lawrence H. Houtchens and Carolyn W. Houtchens, eds., *Leigh Hunt's Literary Criticism* (New York, 1956), pp. 161–63.

13. William E. Aytoun, "Memoir of Campbell," in *The Poetical Works of Thomas Campbell* (New York, n. d.), p. 9. This is one of several memoirs of Campbell written shortly after his death for inclusion in reprints of his works.

14. Pope, "An Essay on Criticism," 1. 298.

15. "Campbell's 'Pleasures of Hope,' " *The Art-Journal*, 7 (1855), 256.

16. J. Cuthbert Hadden, *Thomas Campbell* (Edinburgh, 1899), pp. 45, 48.

17. Peter S. Macaulay, "Thomas Campbell: A Revaluation," *English Studies*, 50 (February 1969), 46.

18. Ibid., p. 44.

19. "The Pleasures of Hope," I:7.

20. Wordsworth, "Lines Written in Early Spring," 1. 8.

21. Wordsworth, "Ruth," 1. 12.

22. "Letter to the Mohawk Chief . . . ," *New Monthly Magazine*, N. S. 4 ([February] 1822), 97–101.

23. William Leete Stone, *Border Wars of the American Revolution* (New York, 1900), 1:377, 288. Stone's original study was entitled *Life of Joseph Brant—Thayendanega: including the Border Wars of the American Revolution* (New York, 1838). In 1841, he published *The Poetry and History of Wyoming*, containing a separate history of Wyoming, with Campbell's "Gertrude" and Washington Irving's biographical sketch of Campbell prefixed.

24. [Francis Jeffrey], "Campbell's *Gertrude of Wyoming*," *Edinburgh Review*, 14 (April 1809), 1–19). Campbell did not take the suggestions of his critics to revise the obscurities and other faults of the poem. Beattie comments:

No author, perhaps, ever benefited less by public criticism. He had an almost superstitious dread of retouching anything after it was printed (1:522).

25. *Scots Magazine*, 71 (April 1809), 280–84.

26. [Walter Scott], "*Gertrude of Wyoming*," *Quarterly Review*, 1 (May 1809), 241–58.

27. In the *New Monthly Magazine* (N.S. 4 [(February), 1822], 97–101), Campbell later defended himself against this charge, repeated by Washington Irving in his biographical sketch of Campbell for an American edition of "Gertrude of Wyoming." Irving felt that Campbell had ruined the poem by following friends' advice and striking out the best passages. George Ticknor wrote in his diary (June 25, 1815) that Lord Byron had told him the same thing (Ernest J. Lovell, Jr., ed. *His Very Self and Voice* [New York, 1954], p. 127). Campbell's letters reveal that he did customarily seek the opinions of his friends about a new work before he published it.

28. [Thomas Denman], Campbell's "*Gertrude of Wyoming*," *Monthly Review*, 59 (July 1809), 239–49. The quotation is from p. 248.

29. [Horace Twiss], "*Gertrude of Wyoming*," *London Review*, 2 (August 1, 1809), 45–79.

30. *Antijacobin Review and Magazine*, 34 (September 1809), 1–9. This quotation is from p. 2.

31. "Campbell's *Gertrude of Wyoming*," *British Critic*, 34 (October 1809), 366–72.

32. Hazlitt, *Complete Works*, 5:149–50.

33. Ibid., 9:243.

34. Ibid., 11: 161–63.

35. Hunt, *Literary Criticism*, pp. 163–64.

36. *Coleridge the Talker*, p. 175.

37. Dyce, p. 208.

38. Review of *Life and Correspondence of Robert Southey, Gentleman's Magazine*, N.S. 3, vol. 33 (June 1850), 618.

39. John Peter Grant, ed., *Memoir and Correspondence of Mrs. Grant of Laggan*, 2nd ed. (London, 1845), 1:214–19.

40. [Washington Irving], "A Biographical Sketch of Thomas Campbell," *Analectic Magazine*, N.S. 5 (March 1815), 234–50. This quotation is from pp. 244–45.

41. *The Writings of Robert C. Sands* (New York, 1834), 1:104–105. The article was first published in the *Atlantic Magazine*, which Sands started, in volume 1 (June 1824), 130–39. Campbell's poem was one example Sands used to refute the assertion of another writer on "Modern Literature" for the *Atlantic* (1 [May 1824], 18–23), who said that "the history, superstitions, and natural and moral features of our country are inadequate for the purposes of poetry and fiction" (*Writings of Sands*, 1:103).

42. Oliver Wendell Holmes, *Pages from an Old Volume of Life* (Boston, 1886), p. 49.

43. Nathaniel P. Willis, *Al' Abri, or the Tent Pitch'd* (New York, 1839), pp. 117–18.

44. Hadden, p. 97.

45. Charles Duffey has pointed out that this line comes intact from *The Sentimental Sailor; or St. Preux to Eloisa* "by a young gentleman of Edinburgh," published in 1772. "The wolf's long howl" is also in "The Pleasures of Hope" (I. 66). See *Modern Language Notes*, 57 (February 1942), 123.

46. [Francis Jeffrey], "Campbell's *Theodric, and other Poems*," *Edinburgh Review*, 41 (January 1825), 271–87.

47. "The Bairnly School of Criticism . . . ," *Blackwood's Edinburgh Magazine*, 17 (April 1825), 486–87.

48. "MS. Notes on the last Number of the Edinburgh Review," *Blackwood's Edinburgh Magazine* 17 (April 1825), 461–75. (Only pp. 461–62 concern the "Theodric" review.)

49. "Campbell's *Theodric*," *Blackwood's Edinburgh Magazine*, 17 (January 1825), 102–108.

50. [Reverend Edward Smedley?], "*Theodric*," *Quarterly Review*, 31 (March 1825), 342–49. This quotation is from pp. 342–43.

51. Although Walter Graham, in *Tory Criticism in the Quarterly Review, 1809–1853* (New York, 1921), p. 43, identifies the Reverend Edward Smedley as the reviewer, Cyrus Redding in his *Literary Reminiscences*, 1:284, says the reviewer was the new editor of the *Quarterly*, John Taylor Coleridge, nephew of the poet. Redding terms the review a diatribe by an incompetent man, but he shows his own incompetence by stating that Coleridge christened the hero "Macbeth" in the review, whereas Coleridge

(or Smedley) was instead drawing an appropriate comparison with Macheath, correctly spelled in the *Quarterly*. Redding says Campbell later showed him a dozen copies of an anonymous "Letter to the Editor of the *Quarterly*" sent him from Edinburgh that attacked Coleridge and his political review of Campbell (pp. 285–86).

52. "Campbell's *Theodric*," *British Critic*, 22 (December 1824), 629–33. The quotation is from p. 630.

53. "Campbell's *Theodric*," *Westminster Review*, 3 (January 1825), 264–68. The quotation is from p. 267.

54. "Review of New Books," *London Literary Gazette*, no. 409 (November 20, 1824), 737–38.

55. [Review], *United States Literary Gazette*, 1 (March 1, 1825), 343–44. The quotations are from p. 343.

56. Redding, *Literary Reminiscences*, 1:266–67.

57. Ibid., pp. 280–81.

58. Hadden, p. 115.

59. Aytoun, p. 12.

60. Tennyson's *Poems*, containing the quoted "Ulysses" (*ll.* 50, 65), also came out in 1842. So did Wordsworth's *Poems of Early and Late Years*, which was as coldly received as "The Pilgrim of Glencoe."

61. *Athenaeum*, no. 750 (March 12, 1842), 222–24.

62. "Campbell's Pilgrim of Glencoe," *The Spectator*, no. 714 (March 5, 1842), 233.

63. [William Jerdan?], "Reviews of New Books," *Literary Gazette*, no. 1311 (March 5, 1842), 153–54.

64. "Campbell's Pilgrim of Glencoe," *Monthly Review*, N. S. 1 (April 1842), 545–55. The quotations are from p. 549.

65. "Campbell's Pilgrim of Glencoe," *Eclectic Review*, N. S. 11 (June 1842), 712–16. These quotations are from pp. 712–13.

Chapter Three

1. In the first edition, the concluding line of the first three stanzas reads: "And the stormy tempests blow." When the poem was reprinted in 1809 as one of the smaller pieces at the end of the "Gertrude of Wyoming" volume, the *Eclectic Review*, 5 (June 1809), 528, criticized the tautology of the line. Later Campbell broke his usual practice and changed "tempests" to "winds do."

2. [John Wilson], "Naval Sketch-Book," *Blackwood's Edinburgh Magazine*, 19 (March 1826), 355.

3. [Jeffrey], "Campbell's *Gertrude of Wyoming*," p. 17.

4. [Scott], "*Gertrude of Wyoming*," p. 258.

5. [Jeffrey], "Campbell's *Gertrude of Wyoming*," p. 17.

6. Ibid., pp. 17–18.

7. Redding, *Literary Reminiscences*, 2:332–33.

8. "[Review of] *Life of Bishop Heber*," *Quarterly Review*, 43 (October 1830), 373–74. The nine-line stanzas of the Danish song contained three short lines.

9. Hallam Tennyson, *Alfred Lord Tennyson, a Memoir* (New York, 1905), 2:502.

10. Irving, "A Biographical Sketch of Thomas Campbell," p. 242.

11. Hadden, p. 65.

12. Claude C. Abbott, ed., *The Correspondence of Gerard Manley Hopkins and Richard Watson Dixon*, rev. ed. (London, 1955), p. 23.

13. Ibid., p. 14.

14. Ibid., p. 99.

15. Ibid., p. 23.

16. [Scott], "*Gertrude of Wyoming*," p. 242.

17. "Campbell's *Gertrude*," *Eclectic Review*, 5 (June 1809), 528.

18. [Twiss], "*Gertrude of Wyoming*," p. 69.

19. [Jeffrey], "Campbell's *Gertrude of Wyoming*," p. 17.

20. "Campbell's *Gertrude of Wyoming*," *British Critic*, 34 (October 1809), 367.

21. Hazlitt, "The Spirit of the Age," in *Complete Works*, 11:163.

22. Washington Irving, *The Crayon Miscellany* (Philadelphia, 1835), 2:28.

23. Wordsworth, "Preface to the Second Edition of Lyrical Ballads."

24. It is worth noting that earlier Campbell had described in prose the effect the launching of a ship had on him—in his defense of Pope's esthetics in the *Essay on English Poetry* ([Boston, 1819], pp. 226–27):

> Those who have ever witnessed the spectacle of the launching of a ship of the line, will perhaps forgive me for adding this to the examples of the sublime objects of artificial life. Of that spectacle I can never forget the impression, and of having witnessed it reflected from the faces of ten thousand spectators. They seem yet before me—I sympathise with their deep and silent expectation, and with their final burst of enthusiasm. It was not a vulgar joy, but an affecting national solemnity. When the vast bulwark sprang from her cradle, the calm water on which she swung majestically round, gave the imagination a contrast of the stormy element on which she was soon to ride.—All the days of battle and the nights of danger which she had to encounter, all the ends of the earth which she had to visit, and all that she had to do and to suffer for her country, rose in awful presentiment before the mind; and when the heart gave her a benediction, it was like one pronounced on a living being.

25. *Monthly Review* (April 1842), p. 549. The article is the review of "Campbell's Pilgrim of Glencoe," in which volume the poem was published. It may also have appeared earlier in the newspapers.

26. Redding, *Literary Reminiscences*, 2:334.

27. [John Wilson], "Noctes Ambrosianae, No. X," *Blackwood's Edinburgh Magazine*, 14 (July 1823), 103.

28. [Jeffrey], "Campbell's *Theodric*, and other Poems," p. 281.

Chapter Four

1. This last line, composed in a moment of inspiration during a night Campbell was spending at Minto, has been so widely quoted that it has become proverbial. In his notes, Campbell attaches an explanation of "second sight" found in Martin's *Description of the Western Isles of Scotland*, in which numerous examples of folklore attest to the validity of visions of the future by seers. Beattie (1:322) notes a similar idea about coming events expressed by the German poet Schiller in "Walledstein's Tod" but feels that Campbell "took it from the popular belief."

2. Redding, *Literary Reminiscences*, 2:137–38.

3. [Scott], *"Gertrude of Wyoming,"* p. 258.

4. [Jeffrey], "Campbell's *Gertrude of Wyoming,*" p. 18.

5. Robertson, p. 157.

6. "Campbell's *Theodric,*" *Westminster Review*, pp. 267–68.

7. Redding, *Literary Reminiscences*, 2:7–8.

8. [William Maginn], "A Running Commentary . . . ," *Blackwood's Edinburgh Magazine*, 15 (April, 1824), 440–45.

9. Aytoun, p. 11.

10. [Irving], "A Biographical Sketch," p. 242.

11. W. Alfred Hill, ed., *The Poetical Works of Thomas Campbell*, new ed. (London, 1868), p. 215.

12. Ibid., p. 218.

Chapter Five

1. [Jeffrey], "Campbell's *Theodric, and other Poems,*" p. 284.

2. The letter is quoted by Redding in *Literary Reminiscences*, (1:304–308), who reports that he did get Campbell to admit that the idea was not original with him, even though the poet had thought so and had objected vigorously in his letter to the *Times* that someone else (Beddoes) would project a poem on his conception and use the very title that Byron had spared to him fifteen years ago.

3. "Mr. Campbell's Last Man," *London Magazine*, 11 (April 1825), 588–90. Campbell's letter also provoked private comments by Beddoes in his letters. See H. W. Donner, ed., *The Works of Thomas Lovell Beddoes* (London, 1935), pp. 596, 600.

4. Cyrus Redding, *Fifty Years' Recollections, Literary and Personal . . .* (London, 1858), 2:290.

5. Hill, p. 131. The "Advent Hymn," which Hill does not publish but Robertson does, begins "When Jordan hushed his waters still." Campbell wrote it when he was sixteen. It has been printed in several hymnals.

6. "Detector," "Plagiarism by Mr Thomas Campbell," *Blackwood's Edinburgh Magazine*, 18 (July 1825), 131–32.

7. Edgar Castle, "Kangaroo with Flowers," *Southern Review: An Australian Journal of Literary Studies*, 1, 2 (1964), 24–29.

8. The sequel to MacCann's story Campbell himself tells when he revisited him in Hamburg a quarter of a century later: " 'He won the heart of a young widow of Altona some years after I left him. He got a fortune with her, and has long been established there, as one of the wealthiest and most respectable of its inhabitants. He took me round a great part of the country in his own carriage. . . . My friend said he was as happy as a man could be, out of his own country; and should be *perfectly* so, if he were allowed to revisit it' " (Beattie, 2:170). Back in 1817, Campbell had tried to obtain this permission for MacCann, but was discouraged by " 'more bigotry in the world than I thought or could have believed' " (ibid.).

9. This motto, "Ireland for ever," set in a shamrock, became Campbell's favorite device for sealing his letters—a symbol of his continuing sympathy for the Irish Catholics. A battle song he wrote for them, entitled "To the Battle Men of Erin," exists as a manuscript in the British Museum.

10. John Gibson Lockhart thought Campbell's "Exile of Erin" and "O'Connor's Child" were "worth more to Ireland than all the poetry of Moore" ("Remarks on the Poetry of Thomas Moore [Extracted from a MS. letter of Baron von Lauerwinkel]," *Blackwood's Edinburgh Magazine*, 4 ([October 1818], 1–5.)

11. Hadden, p. 64.

12. Ibid.

13. Campbell's fellow Scottish poet Allan Cunningham complimented him on this stanza.

14. The *Monthly Review* found the imagery of this poem "Claude-like" ("Campbell's *Pilgrim of Glencoe*," *Monthly Review* p. 550).

Chapter Six

1. [Joseph Lowe], *Monthly Review*, 59 (August 1809), 356–66.

2. "Annals of Great Britain," *British Critic*, 36 (September and October 1810), 249–60 and 335–44.

3. "Campbelliana," *Fraser's Magazine*, 30 (September 1844), 346.

4. *An Essay of English Poetry*, pp. 165–67. Further references are given in the text.

5. Rowland E. Prothero, ed., *The Works of Lord Byron; Letters and Journals* (New York, 1966), 5:25–26.

6. Ibid., 5:164.

7. Ibid., 5:167.

8. Edith J. Morley, ed., *Henry Crabb Robinson on Books and Their Writers* (London, 1938), 1:239.

9. Allan Cunningham, *Biographical and Critical History of the British Literature of the Last Fifty Years* (Paris, 1834), p. 85.

10. Charles R. Sanders, ed., *The Collected Letters of Thomas and Jane Welsh Carlyle* (Durham, N.C., 1970), 2:468.

11. "On Mr Campbell's Specimens of English Poetry," *Blackwood's*

Edinburgh Magazine, 4 (March 1819), 696–708. The "Observations" are continued in 5 (May 1819), 217–31.

12. [Francis Jeffrey], "Campbell's *British Poetry*," *Edinburgh Review*, 31 (Mar. 1819), 462–97.

13. "Campbell's *Specimens of the British Poets*," *British Critic*, 11 (April 1819), 359–72.

14. "Campbell's *Specimens of British Poets*," *Monthly Review*, 90 (December 1819), 393–408.

15. Bryan Braintree, "Remarks on Campbell's *British Poets*," *Gentleman's Magazine*, 129 (April, 1821), 300–301.

16. Hunt, *Literary Criticism*, p. 165.

17. "New Edition of Campbell's Poets," *Fraser's Magazine*, 25 (March 1842), 353–62.

18. "Christopher North" [John Wilson], "Noctes Ambrosianae, No. XXIX," *Blackwood's Edinburgh Magazine*, 20 (Nov. 1826), p. 786.

19. Hazlitt, *Works*, 11:164.

20. Redding, *Literary Reminiscences*, 1:108.

21. Kenneth Walter Cameron, "Emerson, Thomas Campbell, and Bacon's Definition of Poetry," *Emerson Society Quarterly*, no. 14 (1959), 48. The *Quarterly* reprints the lecture for the perusal of modern scholars.

22. "Schlegel v. Campbell," *Blackwood's Edinburgh Magazine*, 22 (September 1827), 347–48. Campbell's reaction to this letter is not known.

23. Redding, *Literary Reminiscences*, 2:290.

24. Ibid., 2:288.

25. Ibid., 2:294–96.

26. Campbell's half of the correspondence with Collier is located today in the Folger Shakespeare Library.

27. *Life of Mrs. Siddons* (New York, 1834), pp. 255–60.

28. Redding, *Literary Reminiscences*, 2:288, 296.

29. [John Wilson Croker], "Campbell's *Life of Mrs. Siddons*," *Quarterly Review*, 52 (August 1834), 95–124.

30. *Athenaeum*, 349 (July 5, 1834), 501–503; and 350 (July 12, 1834), 519–20.

31. *Gentleman's Magazine*, 156 (October 1834), 339–47.

32. *Tait's Edinburgh Magazine*, N.S. 1 (August 1834), 467–79. This quotation is from p. 476.

33. *Monthly Review*, N.S. 2 (August 1834), 424–40. This quotation is from p. 424.

34. *Literary Gazette*, 911 (July 5, 1834), 459–61. William Jerdan, editor of the *Gazette* at the time, said later, in *Men I Have Known* (London, 1866), that "probably a more worthless biography than that of Mrs. Siddons was never given to the public. Campbell had evidently taken no pains with it. . . . It was a very unfortunate and unsatisfactory work altogether" (p. 97).

35. "The Late Mrs. Siddons," *New Monthly Magazine*, N.S. 41 (August 1834), 471–74.

36. "Thoughts and Facts Respecting the Civilization of Africa," *New Monthly Magazine*, 29 (December 1830), 520–30.

37. Campbell, *Letters from the South* (London, 1837), 1:v-vii.

38. "Letters from the South," *New Monthly Magazine*, N.S. 45 (October 1835), 145. This is from Letter II, written originally from Algiers, September 29, 1834.

39. *Tait's Edinburgh Magazine*, 4 (April 1837), 263–65. The quotations are from p. 263.

40. *Eclectic Review*, N.S. 2 (October 1837), 409–16.

41. "The Conversazione, on the Literature of the Month," *New Monthly Magazine*, 52 (February 1838), 280–81.

42. *Gentleman's Magazine*, 163 (January 1838), 70–71.

43. Redding, *Literary Reminiscences*, 2:310.

44. Augustus Ralli, *A History of Shakespearian Criticism* (1932; rpt. New York, 1959), 1:282–83.

45. *The Dramatic Works of Shakespeare* (London, 1863), p. xxvii.

46. *Life of Petrarch* (London, 1841), 2:368.

47. *Gentleman's Magazine*, 170 (August 1841), 115–36. The quotation is from p. 116.

48. *Gentleman's Magazine*, 207 (August 1859), 175.

49. *Athenaeum*, 707 (May 15, 1841), 379–81; and 708 (May 22, 1841), 400–402. This passage is from p. 379.

50. *Tait's Edinburgh Magazine*, N.S. 8 (August 1841), 529–34. This quotation is from p. 529.

51. *The Spectator*, 673 (May 22, 1841), 497–98.

52. [Edgar Allan Poe], *Graham's Magazine*, 19 (September 1841), 143–44.

53. James B. Reece, "New Light on Poe's 'The Masque of the Red Death,' " *Modern Language Notes*, 68 (February 1953), 114–15.

Chapter Seven

1. Irving, *The Crayon Miscellany*, 2:27–28.

Selected Bibliography

PRIMARY SOURCES

For further bibliography see the excellent chapter on Campbell by Hoover H. Jordan in *The English Romantic Poets and Essayists: A Review of Research and Criticism*, ed. Carolyn W. Houtchens and Lawrence H. Houtchens, rev. ed. (New York: New York University Press for the Modern Language Association, 1966), pp. 183–96. Also useful are the *New Cambridge Bibliography of English Literature*, ed. George Watson (Cambridge: Cambridge University Press, 1969) and the *British Museum's General Catalogue of Printed Books* (London: British Museum Publications, 1972). For nineteenth century periodical items, in addition to the Notes and References above, see *Poole's Index to Periodical Literature* (New York: Peter Smith, 1938) and *The Library of Literary Criticism of English and American Authors*, ed. Charles W. Moulton (New York: Peter Smith, 1935), vol. 5. Of some value is S. Austin Allibone, *A Critical Dictionary of English Literature and British and American Authors . . .* (1858; rpt. Detroit: Gale, 1965), vol. 1.

Because Campbell knew many of the prominent people of his day, literary and political, their published letters both to him and about him, as well as their journals, yield valuable insights. An example is *Byron's Works: Letters and Journals*, ed. Rowland E. Prothero, 6 vols. (1898–1901; rpt. New York: Octagon, 1966), now being superceded by *Byron's Letters and Journals*, ed. Leslie A. Marchand, Vols. 1–5 (Cambridge: Harvard Univ. Press, 1973–76, in progress).

1. Poetry

The Pleasures of Hope; with other Poems. Edinburgh: Mundell, 1799.
Gertrude of Wyoming, a Pennsylvanian Tale; and other Poems. London: Longman, 1809.
Theodric, a Domestic Tale; and other Poems. London: Longman, 1824.
The Pilgrim of Glencoe, and other Poems. London: Moxon, 1842.
Poetical Works of Thomas Campbell. Ed. W. Alfred Hill. New ed. London: Routledge, 1868. 1875 ed. with a sketch of his life by William Allingham; rpt. Freeport, N.Y.: Books for Libraries, 1972. First important edition of the collected poems, less complete than Robertson's, with a good biographical sketch.
The Complete Poetical Works of Thomas Campbell. Ed. J. Logie Robertson. Oxford Edition. London: Henry Frowde for Oxford Univ. Press, 1907. The standard edition, although not actually complete.

2. Prose
Books

Annals of Great Britain from the Ascension [Accession] *of George IIId. to the Peace of Amiens.* 3 vols. Edinburgh: Constable, 1807.

Specimens of the British Poets; with Biographical and Critical Notices, and an Essay on English Poetry. 7 vols. London: Murray, 1819.

Life of Mrs. Siddons. 2 vols. London: Wilson, 1834. 1839 ed.; rpt. New York: Blom, 1972.

Letters from the South. 2 vols. London: Colburn, 1837. First appeared in the *New Monthly Magazine,* 45 and 46 (1835 and 1836).

Life of Petrarch. 2 vols. London: Colburn, 1841.

Important Articles

"Lectures on Poetry, the Substance of Which Was Delivered at the Royal Institution." *New Monthly Magazine,* N.S. vols. 1–17 (January 1821–November 1826).

"Proposal on a Metropolitan University in a Letter to Henry Brougham, Esq." *The Times,* February 9, 1825.

"Suggestions Respecting the Plan of an University in London" (title of continuation is ". . . a College in London"). *New Monthly Magazine,* N.S. 13 (1825), 404–19; 14 (1825), 1–11.

Inaugural Address on Being Installed Lord Rector of the University of Glasgow. Glasgow: Smith, 1827.

"Letters to the Students of Glasgow." *New Monthly Magazine,* N.S. vols. 20–23 (1827–1828).

Address of the Literary Polish Association to the People of Great Britain. . . . London: Eccles, 1832.

3. Edited Works
Books

The Scenic Annual, for 1838. London: Virtue, 1838.

The Dramatic Works of William Shakspeare, with remarks on his life and writings. London: Routledge, 1838. 1863; rpt. New York: AMS Press, 1975 (?).

Frederick the Great, His Court and Times. 2 vols. London: Colburn, 1842–43.

History of Our Own Times. 2 vols. London: Colburn, 1843, 1845.

Periodicals

The New Monthly Magazine and Literary Journal, 1821–1830.

The Metropolitan: A Monthly Journal of Literature, Science, and the Fine Arts. 1831–1832.

4. Letters

Besides those published by Beattie, major collections of manuscript letters are located in the National Library of Scotland, the British Museum, the Bodleian Library, London University and University College London, the University of Glasgow, and the Henry E. Huntington Library.

SECONDARY SOURCES

1. Biography (in chronological order)

BEATTIE, WILLIAM, ED. *Life and Letters of Thomas Campbell.* 3 vols. London: Moxon, 1849; rpt. New York: AMS, 1973. The standard biography, long and highly adulatory.

REDDING, CYRUS. *Fifty Years' Recollections, Literary and Personal, with Observations on Men and Things.* 3 vols. London: Skeet, 1858. Genial, gossipy accounts of events and persons, mainly those connected with periodical literature, including Campbell.

————. *Literary Reminiscences and Memoirs of Thomas Campbell.* 2 vols. London: Skeet, 1860. First published as "Life and Reminiscences of Thomas Campbell" in the *New Monthly Magazine,* vols. 77–84 (1846–1848). Rambling and anecdotal, but a valuable supplement to Beattie, especially for the decade 1820–1830, when Campbell was editor of the *New Monthly* and Redding was his assistant who liked to exalt his own virtues.

HADDEN, J. CUTHBERT. *Thomas Campbell.* Famous Scots Series. Edinburgh: Oliphant Anderson, 1899. A short, unenthusiastic biography written in a lively, caustic style. Tries to counteract Beattie's praise while quoting Redding without credit.

2. Biography-Criticism
Books

BELLOT, H. HALE. *University College London, 1826–1926.* London: University of London Press, 1929. Explains Campbell's role in the history of the University of London.

BRANDES, GEORGE M. C. "The British Spirit of Freedom." In *Main Currents in Nineteenth Century Literature,* vol. 4. New York: Boni, 1924. An unprofound appreciation of Campbell as a poet of freedom.

COUTTS, JAMES. *A History of the University of Glasgow.* Glasgow: Maclehose, 1909. An official account of Campbell as Lord Rector, explaining the controversy over his third term.

DIXON, W. MACNEILE. *An Apology for the Arts.* New York: Longmans, 1944. Contains a favorable essay on Campbell as an enduring poet, originally delivered as a lecture before the University of Glasgow (1928).

DUFFY, CHARLES. "Thomas Campbell: A Critical Biography." Dissertation,

Cornell, 1939. Unfortunately not published or microfilmed, this dissertation gives the most complete picture of Campbell since Beattie's. It is
marred, however, by many errors, especially bibliographical, not
caught in proofreading.

GARVIN, FRANK G., JR. *Thomas Campbell and the Reviewers: A Study of
Evolving Literary Criteria in the Periodical Reviews, 1798–1824.* Diss.,
Illinois, Urbana-Champaign, 1973. In *Dissertation Abstracts International,* 34:5909A. Assesses Campbell's place in his time as a writer of
rigidly circumscribed emotional poetry and measures the shift in his
treatment by the reviewers of fourteen periodicals as indicative of the
evolution to new critical standards based on objective evaluation and
appreciation for an intellectual literature.

HEARN, LAFCADIO. "Note on Thomas Campbell." In *On Poets.* Ed. R.
Tanabe, T. Ochiai, and I. Nishizaki. Tokyo: Hokeuseido, 1938. A lecture
on Campbell's lyric poetry intended to encourage the reading of it as
some of the best of its type.

PIERCE, FREDERICK E. *Currents and Eddies in the English Romantic
Generation.* New Haven: Yale University Press, 1918. Places Campbell
in the stream of Romanticism and explains the Pope-Bowles controversy.

SHUMWAY, DANIEL B. "Thomas Campbell and Germany." In *F. E. Schelling
Anniversary Papers* by His Former Students. New York: Russell, 1923.
Recounts Campbell's lifelong interest in Germany—its writers, litera-
ture, history, philosophy, and educational system—and its relation to
his own writings. Mistakenly calls John Richardson the author of "The
Pleasures of Memory."

Periodical Articles

BLUNDEN, EDMUND. "Campbell's Political Poetry." *English Review,* 46
(June 1928), 703–706. Extols Campbell's public spirit in his poetry.

CAMERON, KENNETH WALTER. "Emerson, Thomas Campbell, and Bacon's
Definition of Poetry." *Emerson Society Quarterly,* 14 (1959), 48–56.
Argues the influence of the first of Campbell's "Lectures on Poetry" on
Emerson's understanding and use of Francis Bacon's definition of
poetry.

CAMPBELL, LEWIS. "Thomas Campbell, the Poet." *Monthly Review,* 10
(February 1903), 110–22. An important article, slightly sentimental but
generally accurate, assessing Campbell's achievement as a social poet
("not great, but he has elements of greatness") and speculating on his
reasons for not producing more poetry. Lewis Campbell, editor of the
Golden Treasury series, was a kinsman of the poet.

CASTLE, EDGAR. "Kangaroo with Flowers." *Southern Review: An Australian
Journal of Literary Studies,* 1, 2 (1964), 24–29. An appreciation of "Lines
on the Departure of Emigrants for New South Wales" for expressing and
helping to form the attitudes of the Australian settlers.

DUFFY, CHARLES. "Thomas Campbell and America." *American Literature*, 13 (January 1942), 346–55. Carefully documents Campbell's interest in America and his popularity here.

MACAULAY, PETER S. "Thomas Campbell: A Revaluation." *English Studies*, 50 (February 1969), 39–46. Examines "The Pleasures of Hope" to show that the "genuine merits" of the best parts of this work alone prove that Campbell is "a minor poet of genuine talent."

RICHARDS, GEORGE. "Thomas Campbell and Shelley's *Queen Mab*." *American Notes & Queries*, 10 (September 1971), 5–6. Shows that Shelley imitated "The Pleasures of Hope" in his early revolutionary poetry.

STILLINGER, JACK. "Whittier's Early Imitation of Thomas Campbell." *Philological Quarterly*, 38 (October 1959), 502–504. Establishes Whittier's indebtedness to Campbell's "Exile of Erin" for his "The Exile's Departure."

SYPHER, FRANCIS J. "Swinburne's Debt to Campbell in 'A Forsaken Garden.' " *Victorian Poetry*, 12 (Spring 1974), 74–78. A well-researched article showing Campbell's influence on Swinburne, who was an admirer of Campbell.

[TURNER] BIERSTADT, ALBERT M. "Gertrude of Wyoming." *JEGP*, 20 (October 1921), 491–501. Speculates on Campbell's sources for "Gertrude of Wyoming," forcing comparisons with Chateaubriand's *Atala* and overlooking Saint Pierre's *Paul and Virginia*.

TURNER, ALBERT M. "Wordsworth's Influence on Thomas Campbell." *PMLA*, 38 (June 1923), 253–66. Falsely forced comparisons based on scant evidence and on inadequate understanding of Campbell's opinion of the "Lakers" and of his own Romantic impulses.

Index

162